Comments on other *Amazing Stories* from readers & reviewers

"Tightly written volumes filled with lots of wit and humour about famous and infamous Canadians."
Eric Shackleton, *The Globe and Mail*

"The heightened sense of drama and intrigue, combined with a good dose of human interest is what sets Amazing Stories *apart."*
Pamela Klaffke, *Calgary Herald*

"This is popular history as it should be... For this price, buy two and give one to a friend."
Terry Cook, a reader from Ottawa, on **Rebel Women**

"Glasner creates the moment of the explosion itself in graphic detail...she builds detail upon gruesome detail to create a convincingly authentic picture."
Peggy McKinnon, *The Sunday Herald,* on **The Halifax Explosion**

"It was wonderful...I found I could not put it down. I was sorry when it was completed."
Dorothy F. from Manitoba on **Marie-Anne Lagimodière**

"Stories are rich in description, and bristle with a clever, stylish realness."
Mark Weber, *Central Alberta Advisor,* on **Ghost Town Stories II**

"A compelling read. Bertin...has selected only the most intriguing tales, which she narrates with a wealth of detail."
Joyce Glasner, *New Brunswick Reader,* on **Strange Events**

"The resulting book is one readers will want to share with all the women in their lives."
Lynn Martel, *Rocky Mountain Outlook,* on **Women Explorers**

NORMAN BETHUNE

AMAZING STORIES

NORMAN BETHUNE

The Incredible Life and Tragic Death
of a Revered Canadian Doctor

BIOGRAPHY

by Frances Hern

PUBLISHED BY ALTITUDE PUBLISHING CANADA LTD.
1500 Railway Avenue, Canmore, Alberta T1W 1P6
www.altitudepublishing.com
1-800-957-6888

Extreme care has been taken to ensure that all information presented in
this book is accurate and up to date. Neither the author nor the
publisher can be held responsible for any errors.

Publisher	Stephen Hutchings
Associate Publisher	Kara Turner
Series Editor	Jill Foran
Editor	Pat Kozak
Digital Photo Colouring	Scott Manktelow

We acknowledge the financial support of the Government
of Canada through the Book Publishing Industry Development
Program (BPIDP) for our publishing activities.

Altitude GreenTree Program
Altitude Publishing will plant twice as many trees as were used
in the manufacturing of this product.

National Library of Canada Cataloguing in Publication Data

Hern, Frances
Norman Bethune / Frances Hern.

(Amazing stories)
Includes bibliographical references.
ISBN 1-55153-793-1

1. Bethune, Norman, 1890-1939. 2. Surgeons--Canada--Biography.
3. Surgeons--China--Biography. I. Title. II. Series: Amazing stories
(Canmore, Alta.)

R464.B4H47 2004   617'.092   C2004-902322-5

An application for the trademark for Amazing Stories™
has been made and the registered trademark is pending.

Printed and bound in Canada by Friesens
2 4 6 8 9 7 5 3 1

Cover: Dr. Norman Bethune with his Chinese interpreter Tung Yueh Chian
at General Ho's headquarters in China, ca. 1938

Author's Note
While the author has made every effort to portray Dr. Norman Bethune accurately,
minor details have been assumed to round out the stories of his extraordinary
achievements. This book is not intended to be a complete biography.

To Keith, who didn't insist that I find
a real job when our three children no longer
demanded all my time and energy.

Contents

Prologue

Sacred Heart Hospital, Montreal, 1935

Dr. Norman Bethune showed his assistant the x-rays. There was no doubt that the patient had tuberculosis. Her entire right lung was abscessed.

"She's ten years old and an only child," snapped the doctor. "It's too late for treatment. If that lung isn't removed, she'll be dead within three months."

His assistant nodded, frowning. He knew Norman was right. But he also knew the doctor would be taking a terrible risk if he removed the lung. This surgical procedure had never been attempted in Canada. "Will you try?" he asked.

Norman threw the x-rays onto a table and began pacing the floor. "I don't know," he said, shaking his head. "If only I'd seen her a year ago!"

Norman knew all too well that the girl's parents hadn't brought her to the hospital earlier because they couldn't afford to pay for treatment. Finally, realizing how ill she was, the desperate couple had sought out the famous doctor and begged him to cure their daughter. They promised they would sell everything they owned to pay his fee. Dr. Norman Bethune was not concerned about his fee. He was concerned about the child.

Other doctors would not have risked ruining their reputation by performing surgery on a child who was quite likely to die on the operating table. Norman was not like other doctors.

He began mulling over his choices. If he didn't operate, she would live a few more painful months. If he did, she could die during the operation. Or, she might survive and lead an almost normal life.

He continued to agonize over his decision until the early hours of the next morning. As he tossed and turned in bed, he kept seeing the girl's dark sunken eyes and matchstick-thin arms. She deserved more. His mind finally made up, he sank into an exhausted sleep.

Chapter 1

In His Grandfather's Footsteps

Eight-year-old Henry Norman Bethune stuffed the old-fashioned clothes and bulging envelopes back into the storage boxes. He had found something interesting — the brass nameplate that used to hang outside his grandfather's office. The boy polished the plate with an old shirt and looked at the name gleaming back at him: Dr. Norman Bethune. Henry took the nameplate to his bedroom and hung it on the door. From that day, he discarded his first name and insisted on being called Norman. With the self-assurance he became known for, he told everyone he would become a doctor.

The future physician had been two years old when his grandfather died in 1892, so he didn't remember much about the first Dr. Norman Bethune. But, in the years to come, he would discover he had far more in common with this man than a name and a profession.

Norman Bethune Sr. was born in 1822 at the Hudson's Bay Company trading post on James Bay, a lobe of Hudson Bay, Ontario. The son of a tough-minded fur trader, and grandson of a conscientious Scottish Presbyterian minister, he was destined to become a man of strong convictions. These convictions, along with his outspoken manner, made him a controversial figure throughout his life. Both in Scotland, where he trained and then worked as a surgeon, and then in Toronto, where he taught anatomy at Trinity College, he was known as a man who would not compromise his values.

Norman inherited this trait. He also inherited his grandfather's keen intelligence. Like all intelligent children, Norman was a bit of a handful. At the age of six, soon after his family had moved to Toronto, he slipped out of the house and set off to explore the city on his own. His parents were frantic when they discovered he was missing and called the police. But young Norman didn't need their help. He found his own way home and walked into the house just as it was getting dark.

This independent streak got stronger. When Norman was 10, the family went to Honey Harbour on Lake Huron for a holiday. One afternoon, while the children were on the beach, his father swam across Georgian Bay. Norman was watching closely. The following day, without telling anyone, he went to the bay and attempted to swim across.

Norman was a good swimmer, but the confident young-ster had overestimated his strength. Before long, he was in trouble. Fortunately, his father guessed where he had gone and raced after his daredevil son in a boat. Norman wasn't sure if he was angry or relieved at being rescued, but he knew he wanted another try at swimming the bay. He got his chance the following summer, when his parents returned to the area. He was taller, stronger, and had a more realistic idea of the distance. Much to his satisfaction, he made it.

Norman found danger exhilarating. But other boys his age were not as adventurous and did not want to join him in his escapades. His brother and sister were not eager play-mates, either. They were not at all keen to balance on floating logs or go scrambling up cliffs after butterflies. He soon dis-covered that he had to choose between having companions or doing things his way. It was not a difficult decision.

Being different was not the only reason the intense child didn't have any friends. His parents moved often, so he was never in one place long enough to form lasting friend-ships. His father, Malcolm, had the Bethune flair for speaking his mind, even when it might have been wiser to keep his thoughts to himself. His knack for offending people may have been why the family moved through seven Ontario commu-nities between the time Norman was born in Gravenhurst, on March 3, 1890, and the time he graduated from high school in Owen Sound.

Norman as a boy (second from right) with his
brother, mother, and sister.

Except for Toronto, these were all rural communities
around the Great Lakes. These small towns did not have
libraries where he could satisfy his thirst for knowledge, so
Norman used his natural surroundings to discover how
things worked. Like other boys, he caught and dissected
grasshoppers and butterflies, but his curiosity didn't stop at
insects. One day, his mother smelled an unusual odour com-
ing from the attic. To her horror, she found Norman dissecting
a cow's leg. She was not mollified when he told her he had
found it in a field. He'd wanted to examine the bones, so he'd
smuggled it into the attic and boiled it. After he had cut away
the flesh and sinew, he left the specimens out in the sun to dry.

It wasn't just Norman's reckless antics and self-reliant attitude that alarmed his parents, it was also the way he questioned everything they told him. They didn't know how to handle this son who would not meekly accept their teachings. During an era when most parents believed children should be seen and not heard, they found his constant questions draining. Norman didn't understand his parents' frustration and concern. He was simply trying to make sense of his world.

In an effort to turn Norman into an obedient, God-fearing son, his father used harsh discipline. One day he went too far. Determined to teach Norman a lesson in humility, he pushed the boy to the ground and forced him to eat the dirt. The lesson backfired. Norman didn't feel humbled; he felt resentful. He rebelled against subsequent attempts at discipline and argued with his father frequently. Malcolm Bethune often felt remorse after his outbursts of temper and later would cry and beg Norman to forgive him. Norman grew contemptuous of such human weakness and continued to push the boundaries.

This tempestuous father-son relationship continued for the rest of their lives. Even when Norman became an adult, Malcolm continued to irk his son by not allowing him to bring liquor into the house during his visits. Norman felt this was hypocritical. He knew his father played the stock market — a habit Norman considered as bad as gambling and no more permissible for a Presbyterian minister than drinking.

His relationship with his mother, Elizabeth, was more loving, even though she was frustrated in her attempts to instil religion into her irreverent son. No doubt she compared him to his younger brother, who was far more malleable.

Elizabeth had been a missionary in Hawaii when she'd met Malcolm Bethune. She was an evangelical Presbyterian, determined to spread her faith. When Norman began studying Charles Darwin's Theory of Evolution in high school, she was upset by the "heresy." Norman brought Darwin's book, *The Origin of the Species*, home to study. Concerned for her son's spiritual well being, she tucked religious pamphlets between the pages. Elizabeth firmly believed that every species, including man, had been created whole and had come through the ages unchanged, as told in the book of Genesis in the Old Testament.

One night Norman decided to play a joke on his mother. He crept into her bedroom while she slept and hid Darwin's book under her pillow. When she found the book in the morning, she burned it in the wood stove. Obviously, she didn't think it was funny. Realizing that he'd pushed her too far, Norman apologized.

While Norman's parents failed to turn him into a good Presbyterian, he developed into a young man with integrity and a social conscience. Also, his bravado and desire to seek out the truth stayed with him, as did his urge to push the limits and ignore rules. Eager to get away from the rules and limits imposed by his parents, he left their home as soon as he graduated from Owen Sound Collegiate in the spring of 1907.

Barely 17 years old, he set out for a logging camp north of Lake Superior to work as a lumberjack. He was comfortable in this environment and loved being outdoors. He worked hard and saved as much as he could to pay for future university fees. By the end of a year spent cutting and stacking logs, the five foot, ten inch teenager with steel-blue eyes and light-brown hair was lean, well muscled, and fit.

He left the camp and moved to Edgely, a small town just north of Toronto where he taught in a one-room school. Some of the students were only a year or two younger than Norman so, at first, he had discipline problems. He tried using the strap, but it didn't help. Sometimes the male students retaliated by throwing a punch at him. Norman, never one to back down from conflict, defended himself. Helped by the boxing moves he had learned in the logging camp, he always won the fight. One day, the defeated boys brought in an older friend to act as their champion. The man set out to humiliate Norman, but the young teacher easily knocked him down. That was the end of the discipline problems.

After six months of teaching, he decided that his ambition to become a doctor had been on hold for long enough. He enrolled at the University of Toronto in the fall of 1909. He was 19 years old. He found the courses boring and didn't like living in Toronto; however, he persevered for two years. By then his money was running out, so he decided to go back

Norman Bethune, centre with his hands on his hips,
at a lumber camp, ca. 1911. The founder of Frontier College,
Alfred Fitzpatrick, is standing third from right.

to work. He wanted to work outdoors, and he wanted a
challenge. Luckily, he found the ideal job.

He became a labourer-teacher with Frontier College, a
remote winter logging camp with a difference. He wielded an
axe for 10 hours a day, then taught his fellow loggers — mostly recent immigrants — to read and write English in the
evenings. With plenty of outlets for his endless energy, these

were happy months for Norman. This experience also introduced to him the idea that doctors and teachers should go where they were needed. Norman spent the following summer working as a reporter with the *Winnipeg Telegram*. In the fall of 1912, he returned to the University of Toronto intending to complete his medical degree. Two years into his studies, World War 1 broke out.

Norman was one of the first young men in Toronto to enlist. In February 1915, a few weeks before his 25th birthday, he was sent to France as a stretcher-bearer with the Royal Canadian Army Medical Corps. As a medical student, he was already dedicated to saving lives and reducing human suffering. The slaughter and sheer waste of human life he saw on the battlefield horrified him.

Norman's unit plugged a gap in Allied lines during the Second Battle of Ypres in Belgium. The stretcher-bearers carried a never-ending stream of men with shattered bones, poisoned lungs, or gaping holes in their bodies from the front lines to the aid station. It was exhausting, heartbreaking work. They had to lift the stretchers above their heads to get around the corners of the trenches, often slipping in the treacherous, stinking mud. Sometimes they had to leave the relative safety of the trenches to drag the wounded onto the stretchers. Every time a shell exploded, Norman had to fight the urge to drop to the ground.

After almost three months of service, the horror ended abruptly for Norman. Shrapnel tore through his left leg below

Norman Bethune, age 25, in the uniform of the
Royal Canadian Army Medical Corps, ca. 1914

the knee. Through an agony-induced haze, Norman realized
he would no longer have to carry tortured bodies or breathe
air full of cordite and decay. He had what the soldiers called a
"Blighty" wound. It was serious enough to be sent back to
Blighty, the soldiers' slang name for Britain, but not bad
enough to cripple him. He spent three months recovering in
England and was then sent back to Canada. Because he was
no longer physically fit for duty, he was given an honourable

discharge and a glowing military character reference.

With all the casualties of war, doctors were in desperately short supply, so Norman returned to a fast-track degree program at the University of Toronto. He completed his fifth and final year in December 1916. It did not take long for the newly qualified doctor to find a replacement position in a private practice in Stratford, but his peaceful life didn't last for long. While on a brief visit to Toronto, a young woman approached him and pinned a white feather on his coat. She hadn't noticed his limp and assumed he was able-bodied. In those days, any fit young man who was not in uniform was branded a coward. The young veteran was stung by the implication.

Norman had no intention of repeating his horrific experience in Belgium. Nor did he feel he had to justify staying in Canada. Nevertheless, he wondered how many other people looked at him and thought he was a coward. Norman had his share of faults, but he was definitely not a coward.

Within a month he had joined the Canadian Navy as a surgeon lieutenant, again following the footsteps of his grandfather, who had worked for a time as a ship's surgeon in the North Atlantic. Norman served aboard the aircraft carrier HMS *Pegasus* for 14 months. In February 1919, shortly after the war ended, he was demobbed in England.

By this time, Norman was almost 28. It had been two decades since he had found his grandfather's nameplate and decided on his destiny. He had reached his goal of becoming a doctor, and the war was finally over. He was eager to get on with his life.

Chapter 2
Finding A Purpose

orman decided to stay in London and take a six-month internship at the Hospital for Sick Children. He loved living in London. The British felt an overwhelming sense of relief the war was over — and they were celebrating. They no longer got up each morning wondering if that day would be their last, but the awareness that life was precious and uncertain was still fresh in their minds. They knew they were lucky to be alive, and they lived their lives at a frantic pace.

Attractive, charming, and flamboyant, Norman soon had a circle of friends. Among them was a wealthy Englishwoman who believed he had great potential. Realizing that finances might limit his future, she sponsored him during, and after, his stay in London. She paid for his apartment in an exclusive area of the city, his clothes, and his brief trips to Europe to buy paintings.

Norman had always had an artistic streak, and now he had the chance to develop his interest in art. He sold most of the paintings back in London, making a small profit for himself. He kept his favourites and displayed them in his apartment along with models of bones, brains, and hearts. The overall result was bizarre and interesting — like Norman himself.

His letters home focussed on his work at the hospital and his young patients. However, his mother read between the lines. She was distressed by her son's attitude towards making and spending money, his artsy friends, and the sort of women he attracted. She wrote back regularly, urging him to avoid a "sinful life."

When Norman's internship ended in the fall of 1919, he returned to Ontario and again found work as a replacement doctor. His dynamic personality was as attractive to Canadian women as it had been to British women. However, they were not all willing to put up with his unorthodox behaviour.

He escorted one girlfriend to a dance wearing a light blue suit, red tie, and yellow shoes. Among the dark suits and sober ties of the other men, Norman stuck out like a peacock in a colony of penguins. Of course, this didn't bother Norman. Expressing his individuality was a way of life and he liked to be the centre of attention. His girlfriend did not. She was mortified by the stares and laughter from the other couples.

Despite his flamboyance, people found it hard to dislike a doctor who cared about his patients and treated rich and poor alike. Many of his patients admired him because he not only cared about their medical conditions, he was also concerned about their lives. During a house call to a sick farmer, Norman realized the man's wife was worried about finding time to do the milking. After treating the farmer, Norman rolled up his sleeves and milked their cows.

Although Norman was gaining medical experience, he still didn't know what direction he wanted his career to take. So, when this replacement position ended, he searched for something different. He finally decided to join the new Canadian Air Force as a flight lieutenant in the medical service and spent several months researching the causes of blackouts in pilots. He now had the distinction of having served in all three armed forces without once carrying arms.

Norman continued to think about his future and realized that surgical skills would greatly increase his career options. To this end, he returned to Great Britain in 1920 and took a year of surgical training at the West London Hospital. He then moved on to Edinburgh, Scotland, where his grandfather had also trained in surgery. While working at the Royal Infirmary, he demonstrated his proficiency in surgical techniques. In February 1922, he was elected a Fellow of the Royal College of Surgeons.

The newly qualified surgeon returned to London to take a position as a resident surgeon. After 18 months, when he had finished his training, he sent for a certain young lady to join him. Like his grandfather before him, he was about to marry a Scottish woman.

While in Scotland he had met, and fallen in love with, Frances Campbell Penney. Norman was first attracted to her by her looks, her lilting Scottish accent, and her naivety. She was attracted to him by his cheeky confidence and defiance of social convention — qualities that made him conspicuous among the other eligible men in her social circle. The shy, cautious 22-year-old had had a sheltered upbringing in a cultured Edinburgh family. She was swept off her feet by the brash, worldly doctor.

Norman and Frances were married in a London registry office on August 13, 1923. Frances's parents had serious reservations about Norman. He was 11 years older than their daughter, domineering, and permanently short of money. They also questioned his motives for marrying Frances. Although he seemed to genuinely care for her, she had just inherited some money from an uncle.

The Bethunes spent their honeymoon in Europe. They visited museums in Paris, toured art galleries in Italy, and skied in Switzerland. By the time Norman took his new bride back to North America, they had spent most of her money. The newlyweds lived briefly in the United States while Norman studied neurosurgery at the Mayo Clinic. Then they went on to Canada to visit Norman's sister and her husband in Stratford.

Norman was now 35 and he still hadn't found a branch of medicine that excited him. Although he felt restless, he knew he had to settle down and provide for his young wife. With financial security in mind, he decided to set up a practice in Detroit, Michigan. He anticipated this densely populated city would provide plenty of patients.

Norman chose a busy corner of Detroit for his practice. However, business was slow and he soon discovered many of his patients were short of ready cash. When he treated the local merchants and their families, they often paid with pot roasts, sausages, and bags of vegetables. If he had treated only private patients and had sent them well-padded bills, as many doctors did, he would eventually have been able to afford all the luxuries he and Frances might have wished for. But that wasn't Norman's way. He treated anyone who came to him, whether or not they could afford to pay. As word of his philanthropy spread, he saw more patients, but his earnings were still sporadic. This was not the lucrative practice he had envisaged.

Even so, he and Frances might have managed if he had been more careful with whatever money he did earn. But when his patients did pay, he spent the money on some impractical item or gave it away to the poor. Although he loved good food, he didn't seem to mind when they could hardly afford to eat. On the other hand, Frances certainly did mind; she was not used to financial instability. However, she had never been taught to manage money, so didn't attempt to take control of their situation. Inevitably, their precarious finances put a great strain on their relationship.

To add to her unhappiness, Frances was suffering from culture shock. Detroit was very different from London or Edinburgh. She considered it a dirty and "uncivilized" city. In an attempt to improve their finances, Norman took an evening job teaching prescription writing at the Detroit College of Medicine and Surgery. Although this brought in extra money, it also took up more of his time. Frances was lonely and disillusioned. She was also growing tired of Norman's dominance. After two years of marriage, she left him.

Norman missed her terribly. In typically frustrating Norman fashion, he wrote to tell her that while he still adored her, he enjoyed missing her and so she could stay away a little longer. Whether or not he was teasing, he seemed confident that she would return. Unable to resist his quirky entreaties, she did. But so did all their old problems.

Their financial situation did not improve and, to make matters worse, Norman was often angry and frustrated when he came home. He was constantly upset by the fact that they lived in a society where people were afraid to ask for medical help because they couldn't pay for it. He resented medical colleagues who took huge fees from wealthy patients but refused to treat the poor. With his emotions in turmoil, he sometimes drank too much. Frances, no doubt, bore the brunt of her husband's frustration. By the fall of 1926, a few months after she had returned, Frances decided she had had enough. She moved back to her family in Edinburgh.

Unhappy and lonely, Norman threw himself into his work. He had been a smoker for years, but now he smoked heavily. He began to tire easily, and it wasn't long before he was exhausted all the time. His friends put this down to his hectic schedule and urged him to slow down. However, he had always worked long hours and had never felt so drained before. Finally, he went for a complete physical. Although Norman might have guessed at possible causes of his chronic tiredness, his diagnosis shocked him. He had pulmonary tuberculosis, or TB, in his lungs.

TB was caused by a bacterium that attacked body tissue, especially the lungs, producing lesions. The symptoms were coughing, shortness of breath and, as lesions got worse, haemorrhaging from the lungs. The disease was spread when people with the disease sneezed or coughed, expelling droplets of moisture containing bacteria. If someone was close enough to inhale the droplets, they could become infected. TB was also known as consumption or wasting disease because, left untreated, the patient slowly wasted away.

In 1926, before antibiotics had been discovered, there was no cure for this insidious disease. The only treatment was nourishing food, rest, and fresh air. TB was common among the poor who lived in unsanitary, crowded conditions. Affluent patients with active TB were sent to sanatoriums both for treatment and to prevent them from infecting others. The poor were left to manage as best they could. People who looked after a family member with active TB often become infected themselves.

Sometimes rest and good food were enough to allow the patient's body to heal, but many TB patients died. The disease was almost a fashionable way to die. The pale, thin patients looked pure and spiritual. Sufferers had included famous writers and composers such as Keats, Tolstoy, Chopin, and Paganini. Norman didn't care how fashionable TB was. He didn't want to die.

He was admitted to hospital where he was treated for a series of tubercular haemorrhages. After several weeks, when the hospital doctors had done all they could, he applied for a bed at the Trudeau Sanatorium in the Adirondack Mountains in New York State. Dr. Edward Trudeau had built the sanatorium after he had recovered from TB in the fresh mountain air. It became one of the most famous sanatoriums in the United States.

However, Trudeau Sanatorium did not have any beds available, so Norman was sent to Calydor Sanatorium instead. Ironically, Calydor was in Gravenhurst, Ontario, the small town where Norman had been born. He wondered if he had come home to die. But it was not his destiny to die in Gravenhurst. A month later, a bed became available at Trudeau and Norman was transferred.

He was grateful to be there, but irritated to find he had

to stay in bed 24 hours a day. This must have been stressful on the staff looking after him. Norman was not an easy patient. As tired as he was, he found it almost impossible to lie in bed all day and all night.

After almost a month, his condition stabilized and he was finally allowed out of bed. Soon after this, he was moved into one of the many cottages that dotted the grounds of the sanatorium. As a cottage patient, he was granted three passes a month that allowed him to leave the grounds and walk to the nearby town. When he had used all his passes, Norman and his cottage-mates stuffed dummy patients in their beds and crept out of the grounds, just like young boys at boarding school.

This wasn't the only rule Norman broke. He continued to smoke and he organized parties with wine and food smuggled in from outside the sanatorium. Sometimes he and other cottage patients played cards through the night with the windows draped so no one would see that their light was still on.

Norman paid a high price for this furtive activity; his TB did not show any signs of improvement. The sanatorium was expensive and, although he had an insurance policy that paid a monthly disability benefit, he really couldn't afford it. He decided to leave. He had sold his practice because he couldn't find a replacement doctor to run it while he was away. Like Frances, he didn't particularly like Detroit, but he returned to his teaching position as a stop-gap measure while he planned his next move. Unfortunately, his TB quickly got worse and his next move was back to Trudeau.

So far he had tried to be positive, but now he became despondent. He couldn't work, his condition was deteriorating, and the faint hope of a reunion with Frances had been crushed. She wanted a divorce.

He began contemplating suicide. If he was going to die anyway, he would rather it was quick and painless. The idea of slowly wasting away was more than he could face. He considered injecting himself with morphine and then swimming out into the lake on the grounds of the sanatorium. He discussed this idea with the other men in his cottage. They agreed it would be an effective way to end his life. Fortunately, Norman was not quite ready to give up hope.

He had already started to scour the sanatorium library for information about TB. One warm summer evening, he found a book that literally changed his life, *The Surgery of Pulmonary Tuberculosis* by Dr. John Alexander. He took it back to the cottage and began reading. In his book, Dr. Alexander described surgical procedures that could be used to treat apparently hopeless cases of TB. Norman began to feel a glimmer of hope.

This was the first he had heard of any kind of surgical treatment for TB. One procedure was called artificial pneumothorax (pneumo). In this treatment, air was used to create a space between the lung and the lining of the chest wall. To insert this air, the chest wall lining was punctured with a hollow needle inserted between the ribs. Because negative pressure normally held the lung snugly against the chest wall, air flowed in through the hollow needle. The elastic tissue of the lung shrank to a fraction of its normal size. The lung no longer worked and, aided by an increased blood supply, it had a chance to heal.

Norman was fascinated — both as a doctor and a patient. He read on. Hippocrates had described the procedure more than 2300 years ago. Experiments had been carried out on animals but, until the recent development of x-ray techniques, the procedure had been hit and miss. Patients had also invariably suffered infections from the puncture until Joseph Lister's antiseptic techniques came into use towards the end of the 19th century. The first successful artificial pneumo had been performed in Europe in 1888. Norman read and reread sections of the book long into the night. His optimism returned. Perhaps he wasn't doomed to die after all.

He didn't say much about the procedure at first. Dr. Alexander's book had been published only the previous year. The treatments he described were new and hadn't been performed enough to provide reliable statistics on their effectiveness. Norman spent hours in the staff library hunting for more information. He found very little. Only the most revolutionary doctors were willing to try these new procedures. He widened his search and discussed it with the other men in his cottage, two of whom were doctors. Considering his choices — wasting away at the sanatorium, committing suicide, or trying this new procedure — it could not have been a difficult decision.

As soon as he made up his mind, Norman went into action. In his usual dramatic way, he barged into a staff meeting and demanded to have the artificial pneumothorax. One of the staff doctors pointed out that there were risks. Norman knew them all. He was aware that a needle inserted in the wrong place could cause damage to a major organ, that only healthy lung tissue would shrink, and that patients had only half their lung capacity left to breathe with. He also knew that the air would slowly be absorbed and so the process would have to be repeated, possibly as often as every few days. Despite all of this, there was a chance the procedure would give him his life back. Norman was willing to take that chance.

The doctors at Trudeau were hesitant. They didn't know much about pneumo. However, the sanatorium had a reputation for leading North America's fight against TB, and the doctors knew they would never have a better-informed or more willing patient. On October 27, 1927, three days after Norman found out his divorce had been finalized, the doctors carried out the pneumo. To reduce diaphragm movement and help the lung to rest and heal, they also made a small cut above his collarbone and crushed the phrenic nerve. This procedure was called a phrenicectomy.

While Norman anxiously waited to see how his body

responded to the surgery he painted a mural he called *A T.B.'s Progress: A Drama in One Act and Nine Painful Scenes.* He painted the nine scenes on brown wrapping paper and pinned them around the walls of his cottage. Underneath, he wrote a few lines to describe each scene. They showed his life from birth to his final breath in the arms of the Angel of Death. Upon a row of tombstones were the dates Norman and his cottage-mates guessed they were going to die. Norman's tombstone was dated 1932.

It soon became obvious that this morbid prediction was premature. His recovery was almost miraculous. Within two months he was coughing less frequently and the lesions in his lung had healed. He was gaining weight and could walk without losing his breath. He was discharged from Trudeau Sanatorium in December, needing only periodic refills of air to keep his lung collapsed. His body had healed — so had his spirit.

While recovering from surgery, he had given a lot of thought to the direction his life was taking. The Presbyterian Church taught that each person's life was predestined. Although Norman didn't share his parents' beliefs, he wondered if he had been moving in the wrong direction. So far, his medical work had left him feeling frustrated and inconsequential. This brush with death made him realize what he wanted to do and how he could leave his mark on the world.

TB was killing thousands of Canadians. In Montreal, where many underprivileged people lived in crowded and unsanitary conditions, hundreds died each year. The poor were the most likely segment of the community to catch this dreaded disease, and, of course, the least likely to be able to afford treatment. Dr. Norman Bethune was now a physician with a purpose. He vowed to join the fight against TB.

Chapter 3
Path of Discovery

Norman's first step was to review the current research on TB. This convinced him that scientists were not even close to finding a cure, so he decided to concentrate on surgical treatment. This meant becoming a thoracic surgeon specializing in surgery of the chest cavity.

Thoracic surgery was a relatively new frontier, so the next step was to find a doctor who could teach him the latest surgical techniques. The leading Canadian pioneer of thoracic surgery in the 1920s and 1930s was Dr. Edward William Archibald, chief surgeon of Montreal's Royal Victoria Hospital. Like Norman, Dr. Archibald had survived TB and was eager to advance surgical treatment of the disease.

Norman heard that the respected surgeon had recently set up a research centre, so he wrote to ask if he could train under his supervision. Dr. Archibald agreed, on the condition that Norman acquired a basic knowledge of bacteriology. He did so, spending three months at the New York State Hospital for Incipient Tuberculosis helping with research on lung infection.

In April 1928, he moved to Montreal and began to work with his mentor. Dr. Archibald, a man in his late fifties, was as committed to his patients as Norman was. Their relationship began with mutual admiration. Norman learned the techniques of thoracic surgery by observing and assisting Dr. Archibald in the operating room. As Norman mastered the techniques, Dr. Archibald assigned patients to his care.

This brought a touch of drama to the operating rooms of the Royal Victoria Hospital because Norman liked everything to be perfect when he operated. He complained if the room looked dusty, he complained if a nurse got in his way, and he complained about equipment that didn't work properly. If a surgical instrument didn't work the way he thought it should, Norman would curse and fling the instrument across the operating room, where it clanged to the no longer sterile floor.

However, it was not Norman's nature to complain without trying to fix the problem. After an outburst of anger he often took the sub-standard instrument home and studied it. He sketched possible improvements and, when he thought he'd figured out what he wanted, he asked the hospital mechanic to make a prototype. Usually, the redesigned instruments were far more effective than the originals.

One of his successes was a set of rib cutting shears. Cutting through ribs to get at the lungs was hard work. Norman was convinced better shears would make the job easier but he'd been unable to come up with a suitable design. Inspiration came to him while he was in a shoe repair store. He noticed a pair of leather cutters and asked the owner of the store if he could have a closer look. He snapped the cutters open then closed a few times, wondering if they would cut through bone. He decided that if they were made from steel, with blunt tips and longer handles, they could probably do the job. When the hospital mechanic constructed a pair, they were an instant success, and Norman's new and improved rib shears were soon selling across North America.

He redesigned a range of instruments during the next four years. A particularly popular item was his pneumothorax apparatus, which was used to insert air into the chest cavity and keep a healing lung collapsed. There were other models available, but Norman's was simple and safe to use. It also weighed much less than older models, so became a bestseller.

Norman also invented a new apparatus called the Iron Intern. It was the medical intern's job to lift and hold the patient's shoulder blade off the chest wall with a retractor during long operations. This was a tiring job that prevented the intern from helping elsewhere. The Iron Intern was an artificial arm, forearm, and hand capable of doing the same tedious job.

Soon, Pilling and Company of Philadelphia, a major manufacturer, was making Norman's surgical instruments. By 1932, their medical supply catalogue featured a whole page of his instruments. He had rights to his inventions so received a share of the profits. However, he didn't keep all the rights. To thank the hospital mechanic for his help with the prototypes, Norman gave him the rights for the manufacture and sale of the pneumothorax apparatus in Canada.

Norman thrived on the attention his inventions brought him, but he was not afraid to admit when one of his instruments did not work as well as he had hoped. One technical paper he published ended with a "confessional note" describing several such instruments, along with the reasons he no longer used them.

Compared to his days in Detroit before his stay at the sanatorium, Norman's workload was relatively light. He made a point of resting for two or three hours each afternoon and began to recover his old energy.

He felt his life was finally on track. He was satisfied with his career and was managing well on his modest but regular income. He felt confident about the future and wanted to share it with the woman he still loved. Despite their divorce, he and Frances had kept in touch. Norman wrote and asked her to join him in Montreal. In his letters, he promised he would accept her as the person she was and would not try to change her as he had in the past. Frances was reluctant at first, but eventually agreed. They remarried in November 1929.

It wasn't long before the arguments began again. Frances realized that he hadn't really changed and that they were still too different to get along. She left him and began a romance with one of Norman's friends. Feeling spurned, Norman refused to agree to a second divorce. However, he eventually fell in love again and gave Frances her freedom. Frances married her new love in 1932. Norman, on the other hand, was soon alone again. He continued to refer to Frances as his wife, and professed to miss her constantly.

During Norman's brief second marriage and subsequent divorce, he conducted research, wrote papers, and continued to surprise the medical community with his unconventional ideas. One such idea went beyond being unconventional — it was considered bizarre.

He had been searching for a way to treat a severe chest infection in an elderly patient who was not strong enough to survive a long operation. Based on the long-known fact that maggot-infested wounds were frequently free of infection, Norman cut open the infected area, allowed it to drain, and emptied a test tube full of maggots into the incision. He then covered the incision with mesh and placed a light nearby so that the maggots would burrow away from the light and into the flesh. As he had hoped, the maggots gorged on the infected tissue.

After two batches of maggots had eaten through the

infected flesh, Norman flushed them out. To his great satisfaction, the cavity continued to shrink and heal. A few days later he discharged the patient from the hospital. The elderly man, who had likely been sceptical when told his chest cavity was going to be packed with maggots, was amazed and relieved that the procedure was successful. The incision healed well, and the infection did not return. Norman wrote a paper about his maggot theory and presented it to other doctors. These learned men laughed and joked about a 20th century doctor conducting such "quackery." Norman didn't care. The important thing was that his inventiveness had saved a patient's life.

Norman didn't conduct all his experiments on patients; sometimes he experimented on himself. He had a theory that the body quickly absorbed blood from lung haemorrhages. To prove this theory, he asked an intern to insert blood into one of his lungs through a narrow tube. An x-ray taken the following morning showed that no trace of blood remained. So, presumably, it had been absorbed.

He shared his constant flow of theories with the other doctors — often during lunch breaks. He was so eager to explain his ideas, he sometimes sketched diagrams on the lunchroom walls. There were no quiet meals for those who sat at his table. Norman was a fascinating and energetic colleague, but he could be exhausting, even exasperating. He was so absorbed in his work that he frequently forgot meetings and appointments. Sometimes, he was even late for operations.

As Dr. Archibald's assistant, Norman sometimes gave surgical advice to less experienced doctors on the medical wards. He also held weekly tutorials for the new interns. As always, Norman did this in his own unique way. Jumping up onto a stretcher, legs swinging, he would ask what the interns wanted to talk about.

The students were completely unprepared for this approach. In medical school they had not been invited to "discuss" anything. They had been expected to learn all the curriculum theories and arguments, no matter how outdated they were, and not to question accepted procedures. Norman, naturally, told them to take nothing for granted. He welcomed their questions and enjoyed the stimulating discussion that arose when students disagreed with him.

He was popular with many of the students, but some were shocked by his informal approach and his scathing contempt for doctors who were not prepared to adopt modern ideas. Some of his colleagues were shocked, too. They also criticized him. Norman accepted patients that other doctors had given up on. While his treatments were sometimes successful, inevitably, many of them died. Colleagues also criticized his "showmanship" and his unorthodox treatments — even though they often worked.

A Hollywood actress came to him for a phrenicectomy. She was worried about the scar it would leave on her neck, so Norman positioned the incision in such a way that it could be covered by a short necklace. Afterwards he wrote a paper about the process. He called it "A Phrenicectomy Necklace."

The paper began by defining surgery as a craft and the surgeon as a craftsman or artisan who sometimes had the opportunity to be creative in his choice of surgical technique. It went on to describe in great detail how he had used a bead necklace of a certain length and replaced a few of the beads with a slotted metal bar. He put the necklace around the patient's neck, then dipped a toothpick in dye and drew the incision line on her neck, through the slot in the bar. After surgery, the resulting scar followed the natural crease line of the skin and could be hidden beneath any necklace the same length as the one Norman had used to draw the line.

The paper was published in 1932. Some doctors complained that worrying about a small neck scar belittled the serious nature of their work. To their way of thinking, the purpose of the surgery was to save the actress's life, not to make her look good. Plastic surgery was a relatively new concept. Doctors had begun experimenting with it after the war to try to cover soldiers' horrendous facial injuries.

While conventional doctors were still shaking their heads over Norman's plastic surgery, he was performing another outlandish treatment. One of his patients was convinced that his stomach pains were the result of having eaten a frog. Realizing that the man had psychological problems, Norman knew he would have to make him believe he had passed the offending amphibian. He brought a frog into the hospital, ordered an enema for the unsuspecting patient, then slipped the frog into the toilet bowl. The patient's stomach pains stopped. This incident upset some doctors so much they complained that Norman did not take his profession seriously and was holding them all up to ridicule.

Norman's "showmanship," as well as his insistence on performing surgery quickly, eventually strained his relationship with Dr. Archibald. Anaesthetics used in the 1930s were not as easily tolerated as those used today, and surgeons didn't like to keep their patients anaesthetized for long periods. Norman thought Dr. Archibald operated too slowly, sometimes dangerously slowly. Dr. Archibald thought Norman's technique was too fast and not careful enough. Although Norman cared deeply about his patients and visited them frequently after surgery, they often returned from the operating room in poor physical shape and took longer than normal to recover. After four years at the Royal Victoria Hospital, Dr. Archibald decided he couldn't work with Norman any longer. The rebel was asked to leave. Norman was 42 years old and unemployed.

Although Dr. Archibald had found Norman difficult to work with, he considered him a conscientious and dedicated physician. He was an effective teacher and a first rate surgeon whose skills were known throughout North America. So when Dr. Archibald heard that Montreal's Sacred Heart Hospital was looking for a chief of pulmonary surgery and bronchoscopy, he recommended Norman.

The administrators at Sacred Heart were hesitant at

first. Although Norman's medical qualifications were a perfect match for the job, they had heard rumours about his odd personality. He was also an English-speaking Protestant, which could make it difficult for him to fit into their Roman Catholic, Francophone hospital. Eventually they decided to give him a try, and Norman began his new job in January 1933.

On his first day, he turned up wearing a blue shirt and a loud yellow tie. Bare toes poked out of his sandals. The administrators must have questioned their decision. However, his enthusiasm and dedication to his patients soon won them over. Norman was happy because, finally, he was in charge. His reputation as a TB specialist and a skilful surgeon continued to grow. He regularly had observers in his operating rooms and was a popular speaker at medical conferences.

Although his professional life was now all he could wish for, he was lonely. He still loved Frances, but she was happily married, so he had no hope of winning her back. To mask his loneliness, he kept busy. He operated at Sacred Heart one day a week and also worked at the Women's General Hospital and the veterans' wing of a military hospital. He attended conferences and kept abreast of medical research. In his spare time, he took painting lessons and socialized with local artists. He held frequent parties and invited hard up artists to his apartment for meals. If they were too broke to pay their rent, he allowed them to stay with him.

Norman now earned more than enough to live on, but his generosity drained his bank account. When a fire in his apartment burned all his clothes, he didn't have enough cash to buy new attire. He turned up at the hospital in a ratty old suit and worn out shoes, which he had probably borrowed from one of his penniless acquaintances. A concerned friend collected donations from some of Norman's private patients and gave him the proceeds. The next day, Norman turned up in more suitable clothes but still without a penny to his name. He had bought one outfit and then given away the rest of the money to the hungry and homeless. The Great Depression had hit North America hard, and thousands of Canadians were living in poverty.

Canada's revenue came from sales of grain, metals, pulp, and paper — 40 percent of which were sold in the United States. Factories in the U.S. had growing inventories because they were making more goods than they could sell. Stocks on the New York Stock Exchange were grossly overvalued. When the Stock Exchange collapsed, Canada's export markets collapsed, too. To protect its own economy, the U.S. slapped high import taxes on Canadian goods. Wheat was being over produced all around the world, so the price of prairie wheat dropped from $1.60 a bushel to 38 cents.

To make matters worse, Western Canada was hit by drought. Millions of acres of farmland turned to dust and blew away. Farmers had no money, eastern factories laid off hundreds of workers, and construction slowed to a crawl.

49

Banks called in loans and families lost their homes and their jobs. One in every nine Canadians needed government relief to keep from starving, but relief paid only half of what it cost to keep a family fed, clothed, and sheltered.

The situation infuriated Norman. The politicians did nothing about those businessmen who lived in comfort and paid their workers starvation wages. When the unemployed complained, they were called communists. When they demonstrated, police intervened.

Because of their desperate financial situation, people ignored the early, easily treated stages of TB. Unwittingly, they then infected many others. Although doctors were finding more effective ways to treat TB, the number of cases continued to rise. Norman kept thinking about the young girl he had risked his career for. He had removed her lung and she had survived, but she might just as easily have died from the shock of the surgery. Thankfully, she was gaining weight and getting some colour back in her cheeks. Her life with only one lung would be reasonably normal.

If free treatment had been available, her parents would have sought treatment earlier. He could have collapsed her lung and given it a chance to heal. Norman had realized long ago that the people who needed medical help the most were those who could least afford it. The system wasn't working. He intended to change it.

Chapter 4
Stalemate

In 1932, Norman's ideas about socialized medicine were considered radical. He realized that a system providing medical care for all would be large and complex. He also realized that such a program would probably have to be provided by the government. His cause was becoming political.

He began to sow the seeds of his ideas when he gave talks or lectures. He pointed out that treatment of TB would be successful only when it dealt with two problems. One, obviously, was ridding the body of TB bacteria and repairing any damage. The other was making sure the bacteria didn't have a chance to re-infect. To achieve this, the entire population would have to be screened for early signs of TB. Then, everyone with the disease would have to be isolated and treated, whether or not they had the money to pay for treatment. During these lectures, Norman frequently quoted Dr. Edward Trudeau, who said, "There is a rich man's tuberculosis and a poor man's tuberculosis. The rich man recovers and the poor man dies."

Dr. Trudeau's efforts to change this state of affairs had included building his famous sanatorium using donations from wealthy patients. By providing his services free of charge, working men and women paid less than the cost of their treatment. He also greatly assisted in research both by his own experiments and by supplying cultures of TB bacteria without charge to other scientists.

Norman also did more than just talk about his cause. After witnessing a violent police attack on peaceful demonstrators, he knew he had to do everything in his power to change the system. The demonstrators were holding placards asking for "jobs, not breadlines" and "milk for our children." The mounted police charged the crowd, swinging their truncheons. People surged out of the way, and many were injured in the melee. Norman did what he could to help the injured and, the next day, told staff at the Montreal Unemployed Association headquarters that he would give free treatment to anyone who was sick or out of work.

To find out how he else he could help, he talked to men at the soup kitchens while they waited for their only meal of the day: a bowl of soup, one slice of bread, and a slice of sausage. When he discovered families were being turned out of their homes because they couldn't pay the rent, he helped form committees to fight evictions.

In the summer of 1935, he had the opportunity to attend an International Physiological Congress in Leningrad, Russia. He jumped at it; now he could see whether socialized medicine worked. He sold his car to pay for the trip.

The congress was a chance for doctors from different countries to get together and exchange ideas, share progress, and listen to papers or medical essays presented by experts. Other Canadian doctors attending the congress included Sir Frederick Banting, the doctor who had been knighted for his discovery of insulin; Dr. Hans Selye, who studied the effects of stress; and Dr. John S.L. Browne, a pioneer in hormone research.

Dr. Norman Bethune attended the first session of the congress, then slipped away. He was interested in what these men had to say, so conscientiously read the other papers, but he was more interested in seeing how the Russians treated TB patients. He received permission to visit hospitals and sanatoriums, then went touring.

Norman was not a Communist, so he expected to find fault with Russia's new society. But the more he saw, the more excited he became. Like Canada, Russia was trying to rebuild a ruined economy and yet had reduced the number of TB cases by more than 50 per cent in the last 18 years.

Many of the ideas Norman wanted to put into effect in

Canada were already being used in Russia. Children were routinely tested for infection, patients in the early stages of TB were taken care of in sanatoriums, and all treatment was free. Also, recovering TB patients who were ready for light work could stay in halfway homes where doctors monitored their recovery.

Norman stayed in Russia for almost a month — long after the conference had ended — looking not only at the state medical system, but at everyday life. At that time, most North Americans and Europeans did not completely understand Russian Communism. They knew Communists believed in political and economic equality for all, but were not clear on how this would be achieved. This idea of a classless society that shared in the common wealth sounded unworkable to some, but it did not sound anti-democratic. The world did not yet know how Stalin's policies would play out.

In 1935, when the economy was still spiralling downwards, Canadians were divided in their opinions about Russia's political philosophy. To the poor and unemployed, the idea of being guaranteed jobs and regular meals seemed like a fantastic dream. The affluent saw it as a threat to private enterprise and capitalism.

When Norman returned to Canada, he was offered more speaking engagements than he could handle. Keen to share what he had seen, he accepted as many as he could. His talks and praise of medical treatment in Russia raised a few eyebrows and attracted the attention of Communist

Party members in Quebec.

The Canadian Communist Party helped workers form unions and supported strikes against wage cuts. They also preached against the dangers of Fascism, an extreme right-wing authoritarian movement that was gaining strength in Germany and Italy. They explained that Fascists believed in rule by dictatorship and that this system was enforced by violence, where the strong prevailed over the weak. All property was privately owned, and industry and labour were regulated by a strong national government. Some groups of Fascists tolerated religion; others did not. However, they all promoted ideas about racial purity.

Members of the Canadian Communist Party contacted Norman who, being curious and open to new ideas, began to attend meetings and read about Marxism. He was invited to join the Party, but with a strong sense of self, and a hatred of being organized and having to conform, declined the invitation.

Although work and his growing interest in political ideologies took up most of his time, Norman did not neglect his artistic side. Besides lectures and medical papers, he wrote radio plays about the treatment of TB. He also wrote poems and short stories.

Through a mutual love of painting, he met Canadian painter Fritz Brandtner. When Norman discovered that Fritz was interested in art education for children, the two men hatched a plan. They would hold free art classes for the local children. The classes, which were designed more to stimulate imagination and creativity than to teach painting techniques, were held in Norman's apartment. Norman bought the paints and paper, and the few kids who could afford it made small contributions towards the cost. The men enriched their art program by taking the children on outings to galleries and museums on Saturdays.

Norman painted, too, and some of his paintings were exhibited in a local gallery. Fritz also helped Norman sketch a model city for patients recovering from TB. This fantasy city had everything patients needed for complete rehabilitation, including clinics and workshops where they could learn a craft or trade. Norman fervently hoped his dream city would one day become a reality.

Dreams were all very well, but Norman had to concentrate on practical ways to achieve them. Perhaps with these thoughts in mind, he decided to join the Communist Party, after all. While being a Communist was not yet against the law in Canada, it was unconstitutional and alarming to many Canadians. So to protect Norman's career, his formal membership was kept secret. However, he made no secret of his fight to bring about changes to the system of health care in Canada.

Norman knew his socialistic ideas earned him enemies, but he was shocked when he was targeted for a personal attack. On returning home from work one afternoon, he found his apartment had been broken into. His belongings had been trashed and swastikas, a fascist symbol, had been drawn on the walls. Norman wasn't the only victim of violent attacks from Canadian Fascist groups. Jewish people, Communists, and anyone else who sympathised with the poor and unemployed were targeted. Norman reported the damage to the police. They suggested that perhaps Norman had enemies and showed little interest in finding the culprits.

Far from deterring Norman, the incident made him all the more determined to change Canada's health system. He waded through reports on medical organization. He wrote to experts and government departments in Ottawa. He gathered statistics on the public health systems of other countries and researched their economic and political backgrounds. In December 1935, he began inviting doctors, nurses, and social workers to discuss his ideas at meetings. Those who shared his views formed the Montreal Group for the Security of the People's Health.

The Montreal Group wrestled with two problems. The first was how to provide health care for the poor. The second was how to organize medical care so it was proactive, instead of reactive. Members of the group researched and argued their way through the winter. Eventually they outlined several experimental plans and proposed that these be put in place for a trial period. A plan for the province of Quebec could then be set up based on results from these trials.

Group members sent copies of their proposals to medical, dental, and nursing societies, as well as to other interested agencies. Then, on the eve of a provincial election, they sent copies to Quebec premier Adelard Godbout, opposition leader Maurice Duplessis, and more than 50 candidates.

Norman knew that some people would see government control of medical services as a step towards Communism. He also realized that members of the medical community would worry about losing control of medical facilities or their individual rights as doctors. He expected that the general response to the group's proposals would be hostile. Hostility was better than complacency. Norman's aim was to shake his fellow Canadians out of this state and get them talking about the problems within the existing system. He looked forward to a lively and heated debate over the pros and cons of the Group's suggested changes.

There was no lively debate. There was no debate at all — just a silent indifference. Only a few were interested in the problems and took the group's recommendations seriously. Norman continued to argue his cause, but to no avail. He could not break through the apathy. He was angry that medical colleagues who had supposedly dedicated their lives to helping the sick were content to continue using a system that did not deliver the goods. These physicians were intelligent, sometimes brilliant, men, but apparently they couldn't move beyond a difference in political beliefs to accept that the system was not working and needed to be changed.

Norman became moody and withdrawn. He also

became more difficult to work with. To make matters worse, he presented a paper on errors made by thoracic surgeons. To his great credit, the paper included 25 of his own mistakes. The paper was a valuable learning tool for young doctors, but the medical community did not take criticism well. Traditionally, members of the medical profession protected one another. The paper caused bitter resentment.

Colleagues began avoiding Norman. He lost interest in his appearance and wore the same dishevelled clothes day after day. Friends worried about his state of mind and tried to distract him. They didn't have much success, but an unexpected visitor did.

The visitor was a spokesman from the Committee to Aid Spanish Democracy (CASD), based in Toronto. He told Norman that the CASD was going to send a medical unit to Madrid, the Spanish capital, to help the democratically elected Republicans repel General Franco's fascist attack. The unit needed a leader, someone energetic and able to improvise. It would be a volunteer position, so they needed someone who would be willing to sacrifice financial rewards for the satisfaction of helping rid the world of fascism. The committee thought Dr. Norman Bethune was the perfect candidate for the position.

Norman knew about the situation in Spain, but had never imagined being part of it. He hated war and didn't want to see any more senseless killings. On the other hand, he believed that fascism was the enemy of democracy. Like many informed people, he felt that if democracy died in Spain, it would be threatened in other parts of the world. He thought about recent signs of fascism in Canada and the lack of police sympathy when his apartment had been vandalized.

He began to think about the offer seriously and evaluate how much he would be giving up if he accepted. Doctors came from all over the world to watch his surgical techniques. Many used instruments he had designed. There was still much to be done in the war against TB. But, he was also totally frustrated by his inability to bring free medical treatment to the poor in Canada. The Montreal Group's failure to spark any kind of reaction had made him realize he was fighting a losing battle.

He wrote letters of resignation to his employers and drew up a will leaving everything to Frances. Before leaving for Spain in October 1936, he also wrote a poem titled "Red Moon":

And this same pallid moon tonight,
Which rides so quietly, clear and high,
The mirror of our pale and troubled gaze,
Raised to a cool Canadian sky.
Above the shattered Spanish mountain tops,
Last night, rose low and wild and red,
Reflecting back from her illumined shield,
The blood-bespattered faces of the dead.
To that pale disc we raise our clenched fists,

Stalemate

And to those nameless dead, our vows renew,
"Comrades, who fought for freedom and the future world,
Who died for us, we will remember you."

Chapter 5
Spain: Answering the Call

hile crossing the North Atlantic on the SS *Empress of Britain*, Norman had time to ponder this unexpected turn in his life. He could never have predicted that, at the age of 46, he would be voluntarily returning to a war zone. His life, if not as satisfying as he had hoped, was certainly not dull.

He also thought about the cause he was supporting and silently railed against the short-sightedness of the West, particularly Britain, France, the U.S., and Canada. He felt their refusal to get involved in such a one-sided fight was as good as supporting the Fascists.

Although General Franco had attacked the legally and freely elected Spanish government, he was supported by most of the Spanish armed forces (known as the Nationalists), the Catholic Church, big business, and major landowners. He was also supported by Hitler, who sent airplanes and trained pilots from Germany; and Mussolini, who sent tanks and thousands of troops from Italy. Franco's forces were well organized and well funded.

Those who supported the elected government, the Republicans, were mainly academics, small businessmen, and urban and rural workers who were the backbone of the Socialist, Communist and Anarchist movements. There were few trained soldiers in their ranks. Russia wanted to encourage the spread of Communism, which was Fascism's antithesis, so had sent tanks and airplanes. They also supplied advice on military strategy. Even so, the Republicans were poorly organized and badly funded.

Regardless of the odds, Norman gave himself to the anti-Fascist cause wholeheartedly. He reached Madrid on November 3, 1936, and joined up with Henning Sorensen, a Canadian from Montreal who would act as his interpreter. Henning, looking for adventure, had volunteered for the position. He was in for more adventure than he had bargained for — and it started sooner than expected.

By the time Norman arrived at their hotel in Madrid, two men were tailing him. Before Henning could introduce himself, the two Spaniards tried to arrest Norman. When Henning asked what the charges were, they told him they suspected Norman of being a Fascist because they had overheard him use the word "fascist" in conversation with someone on the street. Also, they said seriously, he had a fascist-like moustache. Luckily Henning was able to sort out the misunderstanding. And Norman shaved off the offending moustache immediately.

At this point in the war, Madrid was a Republican stronghold. There were no violent confrontations between civilians because Fascist supporters had left the city. There was no fighting in the streets because Republican forces were keeping the Fascists troops at bay in the surrounding hills. During the day, this was a deceptively peaceful city, so Norman could tour the hospitals without dodging bullets.

He wanted to find the most effective way to use the medical supplies and money the CASD had given him, so he took stock of the situation. First, he and Henning visited luxury hotels that had been turned into military hospitals. They saw patients dying of shock and watched direct blood transfusions between patient and donor. Only a few of the hospitals could perform transfusions, and donors were in short supply. They went on to inspect casualty stations behind the lines and several base hospitals.

Norman was invited to join a hospital surgical team, but he wanted to be more than just one more doctor on a medical team, so refused the offer. He wanted Canada's contribution, and his own, to be something special. Besides, he had an idea.

He had realized the army needed a mobile blood transfusion unit. The unit would collect blood from donors in cities and deliver it to the soldiers fighting near the front. He explained his idea to the Socorro Rojo Internacional (SRI). This organization, which literally translated means the "International Red Aid," was the only organization running effective medical services for Republican armies in Spain.

Norman told them that a mobile unit travelling to the front and giving transfusions to the wounded would save hundreds of lives. While doctors had recently established the first blood bank in Spain, the officials were sceptical that transfusions could be performed in the field far from hospital laboratories. Stores of blood would have to be carefully monitored, and the delivery system would take a great deal of organizing. Nothing like this had ever been done before.

The SRI took another look at Norman's statistics showing how many soldiers had died from blood loss and shock. It was true that transporting the wounded back to hospitals for treatment took time, vehicles, and manpower. Wanting to believe Norman's arguments, they finally gave in. Excited about the challenge facing him, Norman cabled the CASD in Toronto to tell them the news. He and Henning left for Paris the following morning to buy supplies. The committee cabled back its approval of his project, along with $10,000.

They needed to buy a great deal of equipment and, of course, Norman had ideas on how to improve any equipment that didn't suit his needs. They toured medical outlets, making arrangements for future supplies, then went on to

London to buy a vehicle. This vehicle had to be adaptable. It was to be used as an ambulance that could also carry laboratory and medical equipment. They bought a Ford station wagon and fitted it out with a roof rack, storage boxes, a refrigerator, sterilizer, and incubator. As the station wagon could not supply electricity for all the equipment, the refrigerator, incubator, and water distiller all ran on kerosene. An autoclave, used for sterilizing equipment and solutions, ran on gasoline.

They bought flasks and bottles, chemicals, direct blood transfusion kits, surgical instruments, and blood serum kits for testing blood groups. The chemicals, used to make up intravenous serums and preserve donated blood, were weighed out separately so that each package had only to be added to a given volume of distilled water for a solution of the correct strength. They were thrilled with their progress. The only problem they had was with the Canadian government.

Due to the West's non-involvement in the war, the Canadian government refused to give Norman a letter stating that he was providing humanitarian aid. As a result, he had to pay duty on all the equipment he took back to Spain. Norman was angry; this was money that could have been used to help save lives.

Norman and Henning returned to Madrid in December along with Hazen Sise, an architect from Montreal. They had met Hazen in London; he was impressed by Norman and sympathetic to the Republican cause, so agreed to be the unit's ambulance driver. The SRI found them a large apartment with numerous rooms. The apartment was luxurious, but the only heat came from small electric heaters and there was no hot water. They wore coats much of the time and took very quick baths.

Norman named the unit the Canadian Blood Transfusion Service. Although he had read all the material about blood transfusions he could lay his hands on, he did not have any practical experience of transfusions; so two Spanish doctors moved in to take care of blood collection and storage. They were now a team. Norman was named director of the service, Henning was liaison officer, and Hazen was driver and odd-job man. An American, Celia Greenspan, filled the position of laboratory technician. Two or three Spanish nurses joined them, and a couple of female soldiers volunteered to cook and keep house. The team was also assigned a military armed guard.

It took a few days to organize the rooms the way they wanted them and set up the equipment so it was ready to use. Three days before they were ready to collect blood, an appeal for donors was printed in the newspapers and broadcasted over the radio. The citizens of Madrid were told that blood donations were needed to save the lives of soldiers fighting at the Spanish front.

The evening before their blood transfusion service was due to open, Norman wandered restlessly past sterile equipment, clean beds, and a humming refrigeration room. Now that everything was ready and he had time to think, he was filled with apprehension. All this work and expense would be wasted if no blood donors showed up. The people of Madrid were tired and hungry. Their sons were away fighting. What if they had nothing more to give? Eventually, Norman gave up worrying and went to bed.

In the morning, one of the Spanish doctors called him to a terrace and pointed to the street below. Hundreds of people were waiting quietly for the Transfusion Service to open its doors. It seems that the Spaniards knew that blood was life. The idea of giving blood to save their sons and husbands and brothers had struck an emotional chord. Norman said nothing about the relief he was feeling; he simply asked the staff to open the doors and get to work.

Donors had to be registered then were supposed to be checked for malaria, syphilis, and adequate blood counts before blood was collected. At first, the doctors couldn't find a lab to conduct the tests for syphilis, so the team went ahead without this. They assumed that their patients would rather catch syphilis than die from loss of blood. Eventually they found a medical institute willing to carry out these tests for them.

When the storage flasks were all filled, and there was no more room in the refrigerators, the remaining potential donors were registered, tested, and asked to come back during the next few days. A donor could be called in every three weeks to donate 500cc of blood. After donating, each received a cup of coffee and a certificate allowing them to buy extra food.

Ten days after the service had collected the first donations, the first test transfusions were carried out near the front. Norman cabled the CASD to tell them that the program was a huge success.

Chapter Six
The Fight against Fascism

Norman was elated. He had the blood, the equipment, and a great team. Now he had to consider some logistical problems — preserving the blood and preventing it from clotting.

Blood storage and transfusion procedures were relatively new. Until around 1900, when Karl Landsteiner had discovered the four blood groups — A, B, O, and AB — transfusions had lost as many lives as they saved. Now, with the addition of glucose and sodium citrate to stop the blood from clotting, Norman hoped that they could keep donated blood for several weeks. However, vigorous shaking would clot even preserved blood. Norman was worried that the poor condition of Madrid roads would be a problem.

Miraculously, most of the blood survived the bumpy rides without clotting.

Norman and Hazen had worked out the fastest routes to the many hospitals and marked them on a map pinned to the office wall. When they received a call for blood, one of the doctors transferred however much was needed to heated vacuum bottles, then packed them into a knapsack and delivered them to the hospital.

In peacetime, on good roads, this would have been simple. However, Madrid was under attack. The Fascists had begun nighttime bombing. German planes flew over the city every night releasing their deadly cargo of pear-shaped bombs.

The team was safe from falling bombs during the day, but driving to the hospitals was still hazardous. They had to skirt around wreckage from collapsed buildings and watch out for gaping bomb craters. After dark, it was treacherous. The city was blacked out, so they had to drive through pitch-dark streets without their headlights on. The only illumination came from the orange glow of burning buildings.

Once they got to the hospitals, they had to find their way to the operating rooms by flashlight. The rest was easy. They quickly checked the patient's blood group and transfused the appropriate blood type. If there wasn't time to type the patient's blood, they gave type O, which could be given to anyone without fear of a harmful reaction. The team averaged about three deliveries a day and left extra blood at each hospital.

At that time, Franco's ground troops were trying to push their way into the city; the surrounding hills of Madrid became the front line. Norman delivered blood to casualty stations only 25 kilometres from his apartment.

At the casualty stations, Norman tried to ignore exploding shells and concentrate on his task. He moved from man to man, assessing their wounds. He searched for the soldiers with grey faces. If their breathing was shallow and they didn't respond to his touch, he knew they were in shock. These were the soldiers he could keep alive. When he found one, he quickly rolled up a sleeve, inserted a needle with a tube attached to a bottle of blood, and watched the transfusion perform its magic. By the second bottle, the soldier's cheeks began to turn pink and his teeth stopped chattering.

Not all the soldiers were Spanish. Although their countries did not want to get involved, men from all over the world had volunteered to fight. They spoke many languages, so Norman could not always understand them. They often conveyed their thanks simply by returning his squeeze to their hand. Norman never grew tired of witnessing this small miracle. He never lost the thrill of knowing one more man would still be alive when he got to the hospital.

While they were working, Norman and his team chose to wear the dark-blue overalls that had become the uniform of the popular militias in Spain. The overalls had "Canada" emblazoned on the front and back, and a red cross on a white circle on the breast pocket. Later, they replaced the red cross with a Maltese Cross. They did this to avoid confusion with the world-famous organization that was reluctant to get involved. Norman completed his uniform with a dark blue beret, jammed jauntily on his head.

The transfusion service was still streamlining its blood delivery system when General Franco changed his tactics. His assault on Madrid was at a standstill, so he moved troops into southern Spain and began to attack northward. Norman suggested that they extend blood deliveries to areas in the path of the Fascist attacks. With the approval of the SRI, they purchased and fitted another vehicle. Taking Hazen, and relief driver Thomas Worsley, Norman headed for Barcelona.

Like Madrid, this city on the east coast was still held by the Republicans. While they were there, Norman arranged for an existing blood collection centre to supply blood to Valencia for distribution to front-line hospitals. He also began the groundwork for another idea of his — Canadian-funded orphanages for the Spanish children.

When they had finished making the arrangements in Barcelona, they continued south to Valencia. Norman intended to expand the blood transfusion service along the entire south coast — a distance of 1000 kilometres. By stopping at all the hospitals along the way, he could get an idea of what blood supplies they would need. This was a daunting task. They needed to plan deliveries and figure out how many casualty stations they would be able to keep stocked with blood. They would also need more drivers, doctors, technicians, and blood donors.

When the men reached Valencia at the beginning of February 1937, the news was grim. Franco's troops were already within striking distance of Malaga, the most southerly point of the front, and civilians had been ordered to evacuate. An official suggested that they should consider setting up the subsidiary blood bank in Valencia instead of Malaga. Norman didn't care what the official thought. He had never allowed caution to get in the way of doing his job in the past, and he wasn't going to start now. They left for Malaga the next morning.

The three men drove on, heading straight for the fighting. When they reached Almeria, a small town about 200 kilometres east of Malaga, they were told that they could go no farther. The Republican military defence was collapsing. Malaga had fallen, and civilians were fleeing for their lives. Norman knew there would be heavy casualties, and he intended to get there as soon as he could. They set off again for Malaga but had gone only a few kilometres when they saw the first exhausted evacuees.

At first, there was only a trickle of people; then there was a steady stream. Families, struggling to stay together, were carrying what few personal possessions they had managed to grab in their haste to leave. Norman watched, astounded. These people must have been walking for days.

Norman reasoned that Republican soldiers would be regrouping farther down the road towards Malaga, so there would be wounded in need of blood transfusions. They drove on until, reaching the top of a hill, Hazen suddenly slammed on the brake. A human flood engulfed the truck. The three men stared ahead, stunned. As far as they could see, exhausted men, women, and children trudged along the only road from Malaga to Almeria, their eyes reddened by the dust. Later, Norman discovered there had been 150,000 people in that tortured parade.

Hazen sounded the horn and tried to inch the truck forward without running into anyone. Norman watched an old woman shuffle along, her legs a mass of bleeding ulcers. He wondered how she could possibly have walked so far. Parents carried small children. Older children, too tired to cry any more, struggled along on grossly swollen feet. Those who could walk no farther lay exhausted beside the road.

Scanning the crowd, they saw the first of the defeated Republican soldiers. Uniforms torn, and spirits broken, they trudged along in silence. Hazen stopped the truck again. They were getting nowhere. People were shouting at them, telling them they would be crazy to go on — they would be killed by the Fascists troops.

Norman realized they were probably right. The Fascists had likely already killed any Republican soldiers they had overtaken. To continue would be putting themselves in danger needlessly. There was no guarantee the Fascist soldiers wouldn't kill them, too. He decided to turn around and help the civilians to safety.

They unloaded as much equipment as they could and began cramming the truck with distraught mothers and their children. Frantic parents crowded around the truck. Deciding which people to take first was a nightmare. Should they take a child dying of dysentery or a mother with a two-day-old baby? The child had been born at the side of the road during the exodus; the mother had rested for only 10 hours. When the truck was full, they squeezed the doors shut and crawled back to the hospital in Almeria.

Day merged into night and back into day as they shuttled back and forward. Hazen and Thomas took turns driving. While one drove, the other slept on the side of the road. Meanwhile, Norman organized the truckloads, bandaged feet, and handed out pills. He also gave away the few chocolate bars and cigarettes he had, hoping these small luxuries would be of some comfort. By the second day, Norman could no longer bear to separate men from their wives and children, so they began taking entire families. They also made sure they took the many pitiful children who had been separated from their parents.

There was nowhere to buy food, so the trio ignored their empty stomachs and continued working. They lost track of how many trips they made back and forth, but they knew they must have taken several hundred people; the streets of Almeria were slowly filling with the refugees.

As they were loading the last of the refugees into the truck, they realized there were no men among them. They also saw that these women and children were even more distraught than the others had been. Through sign language, the women explained the atrocity they had witnessed. That morning, the Fascist soldiers had caught up with the end of the column and shot all the men. Disgusted and angry, the trio drove their charges to the improvised hospital and reception centre in Almeria. Their mission completed, they found some cots and collapsed into an exhausted sleep.

They were startled back into consciousness by the wail of a siren. When they staggered outside, they were horrified:

"When the little seaport of Almeria was completely filled with refugees, its population swollen to double its size, when forty thousand exhausted people had reached a haven of what they thought was safety, we were heavily bombed by German and Italian fascist airplanes. The siren alarm sounded thirty seconds before the first bomb fell. These planes made no effort to hit the government battleship in the harbour or bomb the barracks. They deliberately dropped ten great bombs in the very center of the town where on the main street were sleeping, huddled together on the pavement so closely that a car could pass only with difficulty, the exhausted refugees ..."

Norman later edited his journal entries into a report called *The Crime on the Road: Malaga-Almeria*. It was published in the form of a pamphlet and distributed in Canada.

Norman hoped to win more support for the Republicans by raising awareness of the massacre and other Fascist atrocities. To do this, he wrote and presented a number of speeches for North American radio and sent articles to the *Toronto Daily Clarion.*

Shaken by the deliberate murder of civilians, and tormented by the thought they had delivered so many of those innocent people to their deaths, the three men returned to Madrid. With his hatred of Fascism consuming him, Norman threw all his energy into expanding the transfusion service.

Norman had never given up hope that his own country would eventually come to the aid of democracy in Spain. News from Canada dispelled that hope once and for all. The Canadian government was about to pass the Foreign Enlistment Act. As part of the War Measures Act, this would make it illegal for volunteers to fight for the Republicans in the Spanish Civil War.

Even so, there were hundreds of Canadians fighting in the International Brigades in Spain. They organized themselves into an unofficial Canadian section and cabled Canadian Prime Minister William L.M. King, imploring him to do everything possible to help Spanish democracy. The prime minister did not reply.

General Franco and his allies were gradually pushing back the Republican forces. On March 8, 1937, he began a new offensive against Madrid. Norman knew casualties would be high and was trying to extend the service to supply the entire Republican army.

The service was already a tremendous success, but he wanted to do more. He became increasingly angry and frustrated with delays and problems that prevented him from reaching his goal. Intense and driven, he rushed into dangerous situations. When delivering blood, he refused to stay on roads that were known to be safe from attack. He seemed to thrive on the excitement, but Henning and Hazen found it unnerving and exhausting. To unwind, they all drank too much. Norman's hands sometimes shook as he worked.

Malaga had been the first serious Republican defeat. When they reviewed their tactics, the government decided the problem had been a lack of organization. They wanted more control over the war effort — and this included Norman's Canadian transfusion team.

Unknown to Norman, government officials were becoming concerned about the number of foreigners visiting the transfusion unit's headquarters. They also got nervous when they couldn't keep track of the volatile Canadian. To make matters worse, Norman began an affair with a Swedish woman who was working as his secretary. Police thought she was a spy.

Plain-clothes police began following the three Canadians. Finally, they raided the Madrid office and questioned them about the wall map with highlighted routes. They eventually accepted Norman's explanation that the marked roads were the fastest routes to the hospitals, but the

Spanish government decided it was time to take the transfusion service under its wing. They set up a committee to take control of the service and changed its name to the Spanish-Canadian Blood Transfusion Institute.

Norman was furious. He had put every ounce of his energy into organizing this incredibly successful and complex project. Now officials wanted to start giving him orders. In retaliation, he demanded that the CASD repatriate all Canadians involved in the project. The CASD refused, and suggested that Norman, alone, should return. They argued that he could do more for the cause by returning to North America than by staying in Spain. They knew he was a popular and effective speaker and proposed that he tour North America to tell people what was really happening and stir up anti-Fascist feelings. This way, they told him, he would be able to raise money for the cause and possibly influence other governments in the West.

Norman didn't want to leave Spain; but when his team told him they agreed with the CASD, he conceded. The reality was that, having provided the ideas and driving force to get the transfusion service started, he was no longer needed. Other doctors and more politically sensitive administrators would do a much better job of keeping the service running.

However, if he was going to raise money for the service, he wanted to show his audiences what was going on and why the transfusion service was so important. He hastily found a Hungarian photographer and an American news correspondent. Under Norman's direction, they made a film about his blood transfusion service, *Heart of Spain.*

By now it seemed that Norman could not do anything without causing a fuss. The Spanish were still nervous about spies and got upset over some of the locations Norman was filming. He protested that it was impossible to make a film about delivering blood to soldiers at the front without taking pictures and gathering information.

Although government officials were wary of Norman, they were grateful for his contribution. To recognize his achievements, they had already conferred the rank of major on him — the highest rank ever granted to a foreigner.

Norman arrived back in Canada on May 18, 1937, and began his tour. His first speaking engagement was in Toronto. When he arrived at Union Station, he was met by a cheering crowd waving banners of support for Republican Spain. Still feeling resentful about his dismissal, Norman was heartened by the support. He took part in a parade and an open-air rally where an audience of 5000 listened to him speak. When he returned to Montreal, two days later, another huge crowd had gathered to welcome him home.

For the next three months, he toured Canada telling audiences of his experiences and showing the movie. He travelled west, stopping in major cities in Manitoba, Saskatchewan, Alberta, and British Columbia. He included smaller communities such as Salmon Arm, B.C. and Prince Albert, Saskatchewan. He travelled south of the border to

San Francisco, Los Angeles, and Chicago. Venues included legion halls and hospitals. His schedule was brutal and he sometimes spoke to several groups in one day.

He excelled at public speaking, especially when he was so passionate about the topic. So, despite the gruelling pace, he did a tremendous job. He criticized the Canadian government for their lack of support and warned that a Fascist takeover in Spain would encourage fascists in Canada.

He also drew attention to the plight of the many war orphans and encouraged women to hold fund-raising events. The proceeds would be used to create a Spanish village called "Canada" where the orphans would be cared for. The charismatic man attracted large audiences, but donations were sometimes disappointingly low. The Great Depression still had the country in its vice-like grip, and many Canadians had been without paying jobs for six or seven years. Nevertheless, donations to the CASD began to add up.

While in Montreal, Norman had taken time out to visit old friends and colleagues at Sacred Heart Hospital. Despite his eccentric behaviour and difficult personality, many of his former colleagues still respected him as a brilliant, highly skilled doctor. They agreed his work at the hospital had been exceptional, but they did not greet him with enthusiasm.

Norman wasn't sure why they were so cool and reserved towards him. It wasn't as if he'd been in armed combat in Spain; he'd been saving the lives of soldiers fighting for democracy. He couldn't understand how anyone could be upset about that. Finally, he had to admit to himself that whatever the reason, it would be difficult for him to return to medical practice in Montreal.

His speaking tour kept him in the limelight, and his insistence on free medical care sounded suspiciously socialist. His approval of the way TB patients were treated in Russia was no secret either. At the beginning of his tour, a journalist questioned him about the salute he used — one hand with a clenched fist raised in the air — and asked if he was a Communist. Like a seasoned politician, Norman sidestepped the question by explaining it was a Spanish anti-Fascism salute: the People's Front Salute.

As the tour wore on, however, he grew tired of avoiding questions about his political connections. Although his Party contacts had instructed him to deny he was a member, it was not in his nature to conceal the truth. During a dinner held in his honour in July 1937, he finally admitted that he was a Communist. This news hit the headlines. Some people were surprised. Many were not.

This confession did not affect the size of his audiences; the tour continued to be a huge success. By the time it ended in September, the CASD had collected enough money to keep the Spanish Canadian blood transfusion service running for some time. Norman was pleased his final contribution to the Spanish cause had been so positive. But now he had to think about his own future, and that didn't seem too promising.

Although his confession had not alienated him from

the crowds, some of his colleagues began to avoid him. They didn't want to risk being labelled as Communist sympathizers. He needed another job, but knew it would probably be difficult to get employment in Canada now that he had admitted to being a Communist.

A regular job held no appeal for him now, anyway. His attempts to control TB by early intervention and publicly funded treatment had gone nowhere. Besides, that battle paled compared to the fight against Fascism. For Norman, the fight for democracy came first. Spain was not the only country under attack from an extreme right-wing government. The Japanese were invading China.

Chapter 7
China: An Incredible Journey

Norman had been following events in China with great interest. He'd been 22 when China's child-emperor, Pu Yi, officially abdicated in favour of a new constitutional republic. This ended more than 2000 years of imperial rule. The republic soon fell apart and warlords took over, ruling by force and capturing, torturing, and ransoming civilians to raise money to pay their soldiers. Desperate to stop this reign of terror, two groups tried to unite the people into a stable nation.

These groups, the Nationalists and the Communists, were diametrically opposed. The Nationalists believed that China could become prosperous through Western-style private enterprise. The Communists, led by Mao Zedong, wanted to increase prosperity from the bottom up by giving land to the peasants and developing industry through state ownership. With such opposing ideals, they ended up fighting each other.

By 1930, China was embroiled in civil war, and the following year, the land-hungry Japanese seized Manchuria, one of China's richest regions. The Nationalists were intent on annihilating the Communists and both parties ignored the Japanese. The warlords were incensed. Retrieving their land from the Japanese was a matter of honour.

In December 1936, one of these Manchurian warlords captured the leader of the Nationalist Party, Chiang Kai-shek, and would release him on only one condition — that he and Mao Zedong join forces to dispatch the Japanese invaders. The Japanese were now ready to take over the whole of China. The Nationalists and Communists joined in an uneasy truce and turned their attention to the Japanese.

The Japanese were well prepared. The Chinese were not. They needed help from the West; however, the major powers were more concerned with watching the war in Spain. The Chinese and the Spanish were in similar situations. They were both under attack by superior forces that intended to impose their political will on the defeated citizens. In both countries, this would perpetuate the lower classes living in poverty, unable to afford basic health care.

Norman felt the situations in Spain and China were part of the same battle. Through friends in the Communist Party, he made contact with representatives of the American China Aid Council (ACAC), an organization formed by people sympathetic to the Chinese. By January 1938, he was ready to leave for China.

Norman stood on the deck of the ocean liner, watching Vancouver recede into a grey blur. Preparations for his journey had been surprisingly simple. He had no job to resign from and no wife or children to keep him in Canada. His friends were concerned about his decision, however. They pointed out that communication from China was unreliable and news would be slow to reach them. They wouldn't be able to help him if he ran into trouble. Norman, as always, was ready to take his chances.

After the excitement of Spain and his whirlwind speaking tour, the last weeks had been as dull and grey as the horizon. But now he was going to be the first link in a chain of volunteers and supplies to help the Chinese. A young doctor who had helped Norman raise money for the ACAC had promised to join him in China as soon as he could. They planned to take a medical unit to the Communist soldiers in the north.

Norman was eager to get to China. He knew that food production had not kept up with the rapidly increasing population, so many of the peasants were undernourished and in poor health. The Communist soldiers, mostly from peasant families, would be in great need of medical attention. His life would have a purpose again; he would be making a difference. His pulse quickened at the thought of the unknown challenges that lay ahead.

Two other ACAC volunteers were travelling with Norman: a Canadian nurse who spoke fluent Chinese and an American surgeon. The ACAC had seeded the project with $1000, and Norman had raised another $5000 from individuals concerned about the Japanese attack on China. The American took charge of the funds that remained after buying medical supplies and paying for the three passages. He was a heavy drinker and didn't approve of Communism. He and Norman did not get along. By the time they reached Hong Kong, 19 days later, they had already had many disagreements.

From Hong Kong they flew on to Hankou (part of present-day Wuhan) in central China, where they met with Chinese officials and discussed where they might be most useful. Norman wanted to work with the Eighth Route Army (formerly the Red Army), one of the two surviving Communist forces in China.

In 1934, while Chiang Kai-shek and the Nationalists had been trying to annihilate the Communist soldiers, the Communists' position had become critical. Outsiders thought that the Communists were about to be defeated. In a final, desperate attempt to survive, Mao Zedong had taken his men to safety. Mao, the son of peasants, had led the Eighth Route Army on an incredible march of almost 10,000 kilometres over some of China's roughest terrain. This journey went down in history as The Long March. By the time the soldiers reached Yan'an, an ancient town that had been used as a military outpost centuries before, 65,000 had died or deserted. The remaining 20,000 built their headquarters and, gradually swelled by thousands more partisans, resumed working towards their dream of a Communist China.

Norman, always in favour of people standing up for their ideals and principles, was impressed both by what Mao had done and by his determination to rebuild a strong, united China. The nurse who had accompanied Norman, Jean Ewen, was not a Communist. She had come to China for purely humanitarian reasons and would help anyone who needed her. However, she sympathized with what Mao was trying to do and was willing to work with the Eighth Route Army.

The American surgeon, however, refused to work with Communists. Norman refused to work with anyone else. Unable to come to any kind of agreement, the American headed back to the U.S., taking the money earmarked for Norman's medical program with him.

The Communist representatives who Norman and Jean talked to warned them their travel plans would take time to arrange and that they would need an escort. Yan'an was 12,000 kilometres away in a remote northeastern area of the country. The journey would take about a week.

While Norman and Jean waited, they helped wherever they could. They quickly discovered that medical services in the area were woefully inadequate. Norman wrote the first of many requests to the ACAC and other contacts in North America for more volunteers, medical supplies, and money.

When Norman and Jean finally set out for Yan'an, they were not prepared for the reality of travelling in this vast, war-torn country. If Norman had come to China looking for adventure, he was not going to be disappointed.

The first leg of their journey was to take them to Linfen to meet up with an Eighth Route Army official. Norman and Jean left Hankou by train, escorted by an Eighth Route Army soldier. They passed through cities and towns where the blackened shells of buildings were still smouldering from Japanese bombs. Obviously, the enemy was not far away. The Canadians prepared for the worst when they heard the dreaded drone of planes overhead. They evacuated the train, along with the other terrified passengers, and hid in nearby fields. Thankfully, the train was not hit. As soon as the last plane was out of sight, they scrambled back onboard and continued their journey.

They changed trains twice, spending one night in a hut near the railway station while waiting for their connection. They finally reached Linfen — neck and neck with Japanese troops. The city was being evacuated, so the station was crowded with desperate, frightened people. As Norman and Jean followed their escort, elbowing their way against the flow of civilians, they again heard Japanese planes approaching. People panicked and dived for cover as the planes swooped over the station, firing their machine guns.

Norman and Jean ran for their lives and leapt into one of the trenches dug around the station. They stayed there, pressed close to terrified mothers and screaming children, until the planes left. After crawling out of the trench, tired, dirty, and shaken, they followed their guide to the assigned meeting place.

The Eighth Route Army officer was not there. In fact, no one was there. To their chagrin, they discovered that the unit that was supposed to take them on to Yan'an had already retreated to escape the advancing Japanese. If anyone knew where it had moved to, they were not telling.

Exasperated, they returned to the railway station. Civilians were mobbing the train they had recently arrived on, so they had no hope of getting back on. They stood back, wondering what to do next.

Then their guide noticed a small group of soldiers scrambling aboard a freight train on anther track. He pulled on Jean's arm and gestured to Norman. They pushed their way through the crowd, ran across the tracks, and jumped into an open car just as the train began moving. The car, full of bulging sacks of rice, rocked from side to side as the train picked up speed. Weak from relief, the three travellers tumbled against the sacks and tried to sleep.

They woke in the early hours of the morning and realized the train was no longer moving. Hearing shouts, they leaned out of the car and saw the soldiers unloading the rice.

Their escort discovered that the wily engineer had guessed the train, with its precious load of rice and soldiers, would be a target for enemy planes. When all was quiet, he had left the train in a siding and taken off in the engine. The good news was that they could travel with the soldiers to Hancheng, and then find other escorts to take them on to Yan'an.

The commander in charge wasn't about to leave the precious rice behind, so spent the rest of the day requisitioning mule carts from the nearby village and loading the rice into the carts. They had to spend another uncomfortable night in the railway car, then set off the following morning. All was quiet for a while, but then they heard the now familiar sound of Japanese planes. Seeing the line of carts and men strung out along the road, the pilots turned and dived. With no trees, rocks, or buildings for cover, everyone just dropped to the ground. As bombs exploded all around him, Norman lay face down, expecting each breath to be his last.

As soon as the Japanese attack was over, Norman and Jean tended to the injured men. Miraculously, no one had been killed. They continued their journey, eventually reaching the River Fen. When they got there, they found that the junks and ferry cable had been destroyed to hinder the advancing Japanese. Fortunately the river was shallow, and the local people helped them across.

They walked on, stopping only to clean and dress the wounds of refugees trudging along the road. They treated so many that Norman needed to stop at the larger towns to buy more medical supplies. Hearing that the Japanese were only 40 kilometres away, their commander was annoyed at the delays.

Their zig-zag journey was stretching into weeks. Norman began to wonder if they would ever reach Yan'an and the soldiers he had pledged to help. As they neared the next river, the wide, swift Yellow River, they hoped they would find the junks still intact.

When they arrived, their hearts sank. The boats were in good shape, but there were only four of them — and there were several thousand refugees and soldiers ahead of them waiting to cross. Norman's escorts identified the two Canadians as trained medics, so the officer in charge of the ferries agreed to put them on the first junks leaving with the artillery and wounded the next morning. The Japanese were now only 16 kilometres behind them. The weary group spent a cold, sleepless night fearing the Japanese would catch up to them at any minute.

Once on the other side of the river, Norman and Jean set up a makeshift clinic in the only suitable place they could find — a cave. They treated scores of refugees while Chinese soldiers deployed the artillery. That afternoon, the Japanese reached the river and opened fire. Norman, while carrying supplies to the cave, almost got caught in the crossfire. It took four days to ferry everyone across the river. Then, with Chinese artillery holding the invaders on the far side, Norman's party continued their journey in relative safety.

Their next destination was Hancheng, a town with a military hospital. They walked for days, averaging between 35 and 40 kilometres a day.

They were told to wait in Hancheng until the army could arrange trucks to take them on to Xi'an. They were finally getting closer to Yan'an and were relieved that the end of their journey was in sight. They waited a week for the trucks, but made good use of the time by treating an endless stream of civilians at the hospital.

The drive to Xi'an took three days. It was here that Norman and Jean learned foreign journalists had reported them missing and presumed dead following the Japanese attack on Linfen. Norman had already reported his whereabouts to the authorities, so there was little he could do to correct the error. The news that they were safe finally reached the world four days later — much to the relief of the Canadians' friends and relatives.

Norman was getting concerned that he had not heard from the ACAC about the chain of volunteers and extra supplies they had promised. He had cabled them more than a month before and was becoming frustrated by their silence. When he finally heard that a Chinese-speaking Canadian doctor was on his way to Yan'an with the supplies Norman had stored in Hong Kong, the good news was doubly welcome. The doctor, Richard Brown, was giving up his four-month leave from an Anglican mission to help them. More good news came from a meeting with a doctor working with the League of Nations. He promised to supply Norman with more medical equipment.

From Xi'an, the two Canadians travelled the last leg of their gruelling journey by truck. Two months after arriving in China, Norman had finally reached Mao Zedong and the Eighth Route Army.

His arrival couldn't have come at a better time. With little sign of help from the rest of the world, the Chinese were desperate for encouragement. They saluted Norman as he passed beneath their banners of welcome into Yan'an. They hoped this surgeon with his medical supplies and experience of treating war wounds would bring them luck.

They had no idea they would tell their children and grandchildren about the day they welcomed Dr. Norman Bethune into their city. They could not have foreseen he would become a household name.

Chapter 8
Norman's Model Hospital

The city of Yan'an was a perfect place to hide an army. The dwellings, army headquarters, and even the hospital were housed in caves, impervious to aerial bombing. These man-made caves, up to nine metres deep, had been dug out of the treeless hillsides. They were dry in winter and cool in summer. However, in spring, when rains soaked the ancient community, the caves were uncomfortably damp and the pathways turned to mud. To cook and keep warm, the cave dwellers burned charcoal in brick ovens.

Norman wrote that Yan'an was the poorest but busiest and most cheerful city he had ever been in. What impressed Norman most was that there were no beggars. Everyone was poor but Mao made sure that necessities — food, clothing, and bedding — were carefully shared.

Within hours of his arrival, Norman was taken to Mao Zedong. The smiling man grabbed Norman's hands in welcome. With Jean and Mao's aid interpreting, the two men talked for hours.

Mao explained that the Communist forces could never win the kind of head-on confrontations needed to defend the cities because the Japanese were too well organized and equipped. Instead, they were concentrating their efforts in the vast rural areas of the country, where his soldiers could hide and harass the invaders. They were self-sufficient and could continue their hit-and-run guerrilla tactics indefinitely, destroying small garrisons and disrupting supply lines. As the Japanese did not have enough manpower to control the countryside, Mao was confident the Chinese would eventually win.

He then asked how Norman had helped the soldiers in Spain, and how he might help the Eighth Route Army. As soon as Norman had seen how primitive Yan'an was, and that there was no electricity for refrigeration, he had realized he would be unable to run any kind of blood bank or transfusion service. With his disarming honesty, he also explained to Mao that he had hoped to build a hospital, but that the flow of funds he had been expecting from North America had not materialized.

The men discussed the severe shortage of medical

equipment and doctors, both at base hospitals and at the front. Eventually, they agreed that when Dr. Brown arrived with Norman's medical supplies, they would travel on to the Jin-Cha-Ji Border Region to assess the situation and decide where they could be of most use. In the meantime, Norman and Jean would help in the Yan'an hospital.

Although Norman had already seen the military hospitals in Hancheng and Xi'an, they did not prepare him for the conditions he found in Yan'an. He was horrified. The sick and wounded were still wearing their dirty uniforms, and they were lying on lice-infested straw mats. Angry, he began barking orders to the staff. When they didn't do what he asked, he refused to work in the filthy conditions. He stormed out of the offensive cave-hospital and went back to his quarters to think.

Once he had cooled down, he realized he had been asking the impossible. The staff couldn't do what he ordered because they didn't have the skills or the equipment. He got over his fit of pique and went back to the hospital. There was so much to be done; he wasn't helping by giving in to his frustrations about the appalling conditions.

Richard Brown arrived at the beginning of May. Norman was overjoyed to find the boxes of supplies were still intact. He was also pleased to have another English-speaking companion. Eager to be on their way, he and Richard left for the Border Region, a few hundred kilometres to the north.

Jean had gone back to Xi'an to pick up more supplies,

Dr. Norman Bethune, left, with his Chinese interpreter
and Dr. Richard Brown, ca. 1930.

but intended to follow within a few weeks. The two doctors, along with a small group of soldiers, set off by truck. They drove for several days until they came to the end of the narrow dirt road, then carried on by mule train.

At each town or village they passed through, they stopped to treat soldiers and civilians, wounded and sick. They slept and ate with the local inhabitants, who willingly shared what little food they had. Medical care for the poor had been unheard of before the Communist Party began to exert its influence. While the children must have stared at the strange faces of these two Caucasian doctors, their parents must have taken their caring medical treatment as a promising sign of change.

In one village, Norman saw some blue cotton Eighth Route Army uniforms and asked if he could have one. Although Norman was several inches taller than most Chinese men, some of the younger soldiers were surprisingly tall and, with his slender frame, the uniform fit Norman well. It seemed he was no longer the non-conformist who had always dressed to stand out from the crowd. Perhaps he saw the uniform as a symbol of his commitment to these long-suffering people. Whatever his aim, the uniform hardly made him less conspicuous. His intense blue eyes and unusual mannerisms branded him as a foreigner.

They finally reached the first army base hospital in the Border Region and began their inspection. Conditions were much as they had been in Yan'an — deplorable. Again, Norman's fiery temper threatened to get the better of him. The patients were anaemic and dehydrated, and many were dying from blood poisoning. He reminded himself that, as in Yan'an, the unskilled doctors and nurses were doing the best they could with their meagre supplies. Although Norman and Richard were exhausted from the long, uncomfortable journey, they refused to be overwhelmed by the problems at the hospital. They rolled up their sleeves, scrubbed their hands, and got to work.

The poor condition of the patients meant that they might not survive surgery but, for some, it was their only hope. Norman and Richard spent several days operating. They limited the number of operations each day so that they had time to train nursing staff in effective post-operative care.

As Norman prepared to amputate the leg of a 20-year-old, he carefully explained to the staff that the leg might well have been saved if the wound had been cleaned properly by front-line medics. The bitter sense of waste lingered long after the hopelessly gangrenous leg had been buried. Norman and Richard then demonstrated the proper way to clean wounds. After seeing flies swarming around used dressings, then settling onto food, they also hastily explained that the old dressings and the food had to be covered to prevent the spread of germs. Later, Norman wrote an essay called "Wounds" that included the following description:

"*Wounds like little dried pools, caked with black-brown earth; wounds with torn edges frilled with black gangrene; neat wounds, concealing beneath the abscess in their depths, burrowing into and around the great firm muscles like a dammed-back river, running around and between the muscles like a hot stream; wounds, expanding outward, decaying orchids or crushed carnations, terrible flowers of flesh; wounds from which the dark blood is spewed out in clots, mixed with the ominous gas bubbles, floating on the fresh flood of the still-continuing secondary haemorrhage."*

While he wasn't treating patients, training staff, cleaning, or reorganizing, Norman wrote a detailed report suggesting how to improve conditions at the hospital. Ideally, he would have liked to send nurses and doctors to hospitals in cities for training, but the Communist Party did not have the means to do this.

Three of the few personal possessions Norman carried with him across the vastness of China were a portable typewriter, ink, and paper. He put them all to good use. He wrote regular reports to Mao Zedong and the military authorities in Yan'an. He continued to request help from North America, complaining that he had heard nothing more from the ACAC or the young doctor who had promised to join him. He also sent a letter to Jean Ewan telling her not to come to the Border Region.

Norman had been grateful for the company of this plucky young woman. She had been a tremendous help and had endured the hardships of their journey north with few complaints. He would have welcomed the luxury of a properly trained nurse, but felt conditions in the Border Region were too rough for her. He suggested she stay at the Yan'an hospital as head nurse. He never saw Jean again.

Norman and Richard could have kept busy for much

longer at the Border Region hospital but Richard's time was limited and they both wanted to get closer to the front line. They left by truck at the end of May and, with more stops to treat those in need along the way, drove through the Wu Tai Mountains, home of one of the five Buddhist sacred mountains and hundreds of monasteries and temples. They arrived at Jingangku, the headquarters of the Border Region, in June.

Again, Norman's small party was welcomed by cheering Chinese lining the main street. Word of this Canadian doctor who had come to help them in their time of great need spreading.

Norman and Richard were anxious to visit the hospital, a day's journey by horse. They were told they could not go without an escort, so General Nieh Jung-chen, the Commander-in-Chief of the Region, accompanied them. During the ride, with Richard acting as interpreter, the general told Norman about some of the problems facing the army.

The Communist army was trying to improve the battered economy, but in recent years exports of silk and tea had lost ground to competitors in Japan and India. Foreign demand had plummeted due to the Great Depression. Peasants were caught in an ecological crisis for a whole list of reasons, including soil exhaustion, primitive technology, and exploitive tenancy agreements.

They were barely growing enough food to feed everyone and had seen little improvement in living conditions in more than 200 years. They were mostly illiterate, especially the women, and were suspicious of land redistribution schemes. Mao was trying to teach everyone to read and write but, with no money to spare, progress was slow.

The Army was made up of young men and women from the villages and towns scattered throughout the vast area. Communications were poor and military equipment was scarce. Whenever their soldiers attacked small pockets of the enemy, they struck swiftly and captured whatever supplies and equipment they could carry before disappearing back into the hills.

Their greatest fear was of being wounded. Unlike the Japanese, who had well-equipped medical divisions and trained medics, the most the Chinese could hope for was some basic first aid. They had no illusions about the outcome of a serious wound — death from blood loss or blood poisoning.

With typical Chinese delicacy, General Nieh did not mention the problem Norman was already aware of: that Western governments were too afraid of Communism to support the Communist fight against the Japanese.

The hospital they rode to that day did not even have a common building. Instead, the patients were housed in peasants' huts throughout the town. Within days, the two doctors began operating on the most seriously injured patients. They also gave daily lectures to the staff who, again, were mostly untrained.

As soon as he had attended to the immediate problems,

Norman constructed an operating room in an unused building. He dreamed of providing these needy and long-suffering people with a proper hospital. Not a muddy cave or a peasant hut, but a building with beds and other essential equipment. A building that could at least be kept clean, if not sterile. Unfortunately, without the promised support from the ACAC, he did not have the financial resources. In fact, he did not even have enough money for his own basic needs. He was in the embarrassing position of having to rely on the very limited resources of the Chinese.

Norman presented his idea for a permanent hospital to General Nieh. The pragmatic soldier was not keen on the idea. He argued that the Japanese would destroy any hospital in their path, so money and precious building materials would be wasted. Naturally, Norman did not give up on his idea. He was sure that a proper hospital was the key to providing better medical care. He used his considerable powers of persuasion on anyone who would listen. Eventually, the council in charge of such matters directed General Nieh to approve Norman's idea.

Norman had already chosen the location for his Model Hospital — a quiet place that would not be of interest to the Japanese. He intended to build it in part of a Buddhist temple near the village of Songyankou, an idyllic spot within sight of the Great Wall of China. While visiting the site, he walked among the trees and gazed out at the distant mountains. The temple priests were chanting their prayers, accompanied by bells and gongs. The scent of joss sticks wafted through the air. He closed his eyes and breathed deeply, feeling a healing peace wash over him.

By now, Dr. Richard Brown's leave had come to an end and he returned to his mission. Norman missed his only English-speaking companion, but he filled the void by staying busy. All the villagers helped fit out and furnish the hospital. While the men constructed the inside, the women stuffed mattresses with straw and sewed blankets and sheets.

Norman intended to train staff at the hospital, as well as care for the sick and wounded. In between treating patients and organizing construction of the hospital, he wrote a textbook for the medical course he was planning to teach. Villagers marvelled at the energy of this tireless man.

He also continued to write articles for newspapers in North America. He sent these to an American in Yan'an who forwarded them for mailing overseas. He saw a parallel between the centuries-old medical neglect of the poor in China and the neglect of the poor in Canada. He wanted Westerners to understand how socialized medicine could change this state of affairs, and what the Communists were trying to do. He also hoped that payment for the articles would support him and his medical projects.

His thoughts on what was happening in Asia surfaced in essays such as "Wounds" published in Canada and America the following year. After describing the horrific wounds, he wrote about the men who made them:

"Is it possible that a few rich men, a small class of men, have persuaded a million poor men to attack, and attempt to destroy, another million men as poor as they? So that the rich may be richer still? Terrible thought! How did they persuade these poor men to come to China? By telling them the truth? No, they would never have come if they had known the truth. Did they dare to tell these workmen that the rich only wanted cheaper raw materials, more markets and more profit? No, they told them that this brutal war was 'The Destiny of the Race,' it was for the 'Glory of the Emperor,' it was for the 'Honour of the State,' it was for their 'King and Country.'"

After several weeks of enthusiastic work, Norman's Model Hospital was finally ready. The hospital was decorated with banners and, on September 15, 1938, was officially opened. Through an interpreter, Norman gave a speech and thanked everyone for their contribution. Also, as he so often did, he urged the staff to constantly look for better ways to do their jobs.

Norman was about to begin his training program at the hospital but, a few days after the opening ceremony, the Japanese launched a heavy attack in a neighbouring province. He was needed at the front. The training program would have to wait.

Norman set out with a small group of medics, feeling

satisfied that his efforts were beginning to come to fruition. While he was away, a Japanese division reached the peaceful village of Songyankou. The hospital staff had sufficient warning to evacuate the patients, but the Japanese soldiers destroyed the hospital.

Norman was devastated when he heard the news. He had to face the fact that General Nieh had been right. He swallowed his disappointment and considered his next move.

After much thought, he decided on a plan he had considered earlier. He would train mobile medical units that could reach the front lines quickly. Since arriving in the Jin-Cha-Ji Border Region, he had seen too many soldiers with gangrene and blood poisoning. Treating the wounded within a few hours of injury would greatly reduce the number of amputated limbs and lost lives. Norman put together a "prototype" unit, then waited to be summoned to the next battle.

Chapter 9
A Man of
the People

By November, Norman and his prototype unit had been called to the front line in Hebei province. The men — Norman, three trainee doctors, and an assistant — set up their "operating room" in a small open temple with a frame, but no walls. Their roof was a sheet draped over the beams to keep out the snow.

They crowded around a log fire, trying to stay warm until their first patients were brought in from the battlefield, 20 kilometres away. They didn't have to wait long. The four doctors and their assistant operated steadily for 40 hours. Finally, two extra doctors arrived to spell them off. The team slept for a few hours then got back to work.

Like the rest of his team, Norman was exhausted by the time the last patient had been bandaged and lifted down from the makeshift operating table. Despite being cold, hungry, and tired, Norman felt satisfied. He was sure most of these soldiers would be recovering by the time he examined them a couple of days later at the base hospital. His idea for mobile medical units was feasible.

Now that he again had a purpose, he threw all his energy into planning more units. In Yangjiazhuang, his new headquarters, he trained representatives from each of the Border Region subdivisions, showing them what their unit duties would be. These trained medics then went back to their home subdivision and trained others.

Norman spent the next four months touring the Border Region hospitals as part of a mobile 18-person medical unit. They dressed as peasants and rode at night for safety, Norman on a horse that had been captured from the Japanese. At each hospital, he suggested improvements and operated on the more serious cases, explaining and teaching other doctors as he did so.

Because he was constantly on the move, medical equipment had to be light and mobile. He designed a wooden case that would fit on the back of a mule. Inside, he could pack supplies for 100 operations, 500 dressings, and 500 prescriptions. He designed another mule pack that opened into an operating table.

Norman also had to use his ingenuity to find blood

donors. Transfusions had to be given directly from donor to patient. The Chinese in this remote corner of the country did not understand how blood transfusions worked and were afraid to give blood. With a hint of his old showmanship, Norman selected a wounded soldier who had his blood group and held a demonstration.

He gathered the villagers and explained what he was going to do. He then rolled up his sleeve, lay beside the pale, unconscious patient, and had a needle inserted into his vein. As Norman's blood flowed into the patient, the colour came back into his face and he opened his eyes. Just as Norman had hoped, the little miracle made a huge impression on the villagers. They could hardly believe how quickly the patient had "come back from the dead." When Norman asked the villagers to have their blood typed, one by one they agreed.

News of the demonstration spread. If the doctor was prepared to give his own blood, then it must be safe. Norman no longer had any trouble finding blood donors.

The reputation of this foreign doctor was spreading and boosting spirits. He was not like other foreigners. He worked long hours, refusing to rest until all the wounded had been taken care of, and was never too proud to help with non-medical tasks. People repeated stories of how this great doctor had sewn saddlebags, made a tin cooking stove, and pushed a truck out of the mud alongside his comrades. Soldiers began to realize that the quality of medical care was improving. They were no longer convinced they would die if they were wounded.

Norman had treated countless soldiers by now, but he also treated anyone else who needed attention. One mother couldn't thank him enough after he repaired her daughter's harelip so that she could speak properly.

People began to revere this strange foreigner, despite his Western "rudeness." In a culture where plain speaking was impolite, people were shocked by his frank attitude, even though his interpreter softened the bluntness of his words. His saving grace was that he never asked anyone to do anything he wouldn't do himself. This "comradely" attitude, as well as his expertise and dedication, earned him their admiration and gratitude.

In his constant travels, he slept where the people slept and ate what the people ate — boiled millet with cabbage and perhaps some meat or eggs. These meagre meals were always accompanied by tea that Norman found slightly bitter without milk and sugar — two of life's little pleasures he was beginning to miss.

Villagers, as well as the soldiers, began protecting their benefactor in any way they could. On one occasion they saved Norman's entire unit from capture. While Norman was working in a makeshift operating room, 400 Japanese soldiers were seen approaching. One villager burst into the operating room to warn Norman, while others helped carry the patients to safety. Those patients who couldn't be moved were hidden under piles of straw. Within 10 minutes, Norman and his team had packed up their equipment and escaped.

By now Norman had been appointed medical advisor of the Jin-Cha-Ji Border Region. He was the only doctor with a formal medical training for hundreds of kilometres. The responsibility weighed heavily at times.

Norman travelled constantly throughout the winter of 1938 and into the spring. The warmer weather made life more comfortable, but then he had to deal with the mud. With summer came the choking dust and the return of the ever-present flies. When he arrived at each new village, he attended to patients before allowing himself to rest.

Supplies were a constant concern. One afternoon he had to saw off a man's leg using a carpenter's saw. Sometimes he ran out of anaesthetic and had to operate without it, gritting his teeth as patients cried out in pain.

After enemy attacks, there were so many wounded soldiers and civilians, Norman sometimes operated for two or three days at a time. He managed this feat by taking 15-minute breaks when he could no longer carry on. He didn't stop until every patient had been treated. During periods of relative calm, he found time to write in his journal and fill out reports to General Nieh.

Months passed with only his interpreter to talk to and Norman began longing for English conversation. He also yearned for music and good food. He wrote letters to friends, often signed "Beth," begging for new English books. He had read the few he had with him over and over. He waited in anticipation for replies, but none came. He resigned himself to the fact that his letters were probably not getting out of China. The few letters that did reach him had already been opened and were falling apart. He never did find out that the American government had refused to issue a passport for the young American doctor who had planned to join him.

He had no radio and saw no newspapers. He was completely isolated from the outside world. He barely had time to think of Spain, and had no way of knowing that General Franco had finally won.

Despite the hardships, Norman felt fulfilled — even happy. He was needed. He had endless work to keep him busy and the people gave him everything he required. They were even giving him the money to rebuild his hospital. Norman was thrilled. The Chinese were eager to learn, and a proper teaching facility would help with the mammoth task of training sufficient medical staff.

By the start of the summer, Norman had chosen a site for a new hospital, this time in Niuyankou far from the fighting. He had also outlined a training program for the hospital's medical school. The building was finished in September 1939.

Norman was excited about his new venture, but he was running out of energy. His staff began to worry about their gaunt doctor. Living the life of a superhero had taken its toll. Norman was now 49, underfed, and overworked. He'd been deaf in one ear for three months, his teeth ached, and he needed new glasses.

The longing for life's finer things became more intense. He could barely remember what it felt like to sleep in a soft bed; have a long, hot shower; or wear a clean, crisp shirt. He began dreaming of roast beef, apple pie, ice cream — and coffee.

He had now been in China for 18 months and he desperately needed a break. He decided to take a brief trip home to Canada. He would take care of his health needs and gain a few pounds. He would also raise the money to equip his Model Hospital and see if he could find teaching staff to help him with the training. He had no idea that Europe was on the verge of World War II.

He made arrangements to leave China in October, then began an inspection tour of the base hospitals to make sure that everything would run smoothly while he was away. As usual, he performed surgery. During one simple operation, he cut his finger. This was a common occurrence, so he was not unduly concerned. However, before this cut had healed, Norman operated on a soldier with a highly infectious head wound. He was not wearing rubber gloves. Norman preferred to operate without them, anyway, but in this instance he had no choice; the hospital did not have any.

Three days later, Norman's finger was swollen and he had a fever. His fingers had been infected before, but they had always healed. If he had been well nourished and in good health, he might have fought off this infection, too. In his weakened state, blood poisoning quickly spread through his body. There were no antibiotics to work their magic. The lethal condition he had worked so hard to prevent in others was going to claim him.

He knew he would never see Canada again. Between bouts of vomiting, fever, and chills he tried to supervise the medical unit from his stretcher. Painkillers were of little help; he suffered the agony he had watched so many others endure. Dr. Norman Bethune died in a hut in Huangshikou in the early hours of November 12, 1939.

He was a long way from home, but he wasn't alone. He had given his comrades everything he had; in exchange they gave him their respect, admiration, and love. The soldiers and civilians were distraught. They filed silently past him, unashamed of their tears. They took his body to a small village, four days away, where it would be safe from the Japanese.

The sad news spread through the Eighth Route Army. When Mao Zedong heard, he wrote a eulogy *In Memory of Norman Bethune,* in which he praised Norman for his selflessness and his great dedication to the people. In January, they moved the coffin to Zhucheng and buried it on the hillside, marking the site with a tomb. Thousands came to say goodbye to their hero.

A few months later, Japanese found the tomb and destroyed it. After they had gone, the Chinese restored the site but, in 1952, Norman's remains were moved to a memorial park in Shijiazhuang. The park is dedicated to the memory of the 25,000 Chinese who lost their lives fighting the Nationalists and the Japanese.

Thousands of Chinese and foreigners visit Norman's tomb each year. They also visit the nearby museum where his few personal effects, including his typewriter, are on display. Beside the museum is the most fitting memorial of all: The Norman Bethune International Peace Hospital, a modern, functioning Model Hospital. Norman's dream had finally been realized.

Epilogue

Canadians reacted quietly to the news of Norman's death. While his body was lying in state at Zhucheng, the Canadian government passed an amendment to the War Measures Act banning the Communist Party of Canada and making it unlawful for Canadians to belong. Norman's embrace of Communism was embarrassing to say the least, and, officially, Canada tried to ignore him.

In the years following his death, however, relations between Canada and China improved. Chinese visitors and officials wanted to see Norman's birthplace in Gravenhurst, Ontario. They wanted to go into the house where he had been born — the old Presbyterian manse. By 1973, Pierre Trudeau's Liberal government felt obliged to acknowledge what Norman had done. They bought the old house, restored it to look as it had when the Bethunes lived there, and made it into a museum. It opened in 1976.

China and Canada jointly issued stamps of Norman in 1990. The Royal Canadian Mint struck a 1997 five-dollar coin showing him riding a horse in a caravan of soldiers and mules. In August 2000, Governor General Adrienne Clarkson unveiled a bronze statue of Norman in downtown Gravenhurst.

Epilogue

Almost half a century after his death, however, his 1998 induction into the Canadian Medical Hall of Fame continued to stir up controversy. Some Canadians opposed his induction. Their reasons were that he had supported a political party that intentionally starved millions of people, and that he had deserted Canada and saved the lives of Chinese whose sons may well have later fought against Canadians. They also claimed that Norman would have been forgotten by the Chinese if the Communists hadn't eventually succeeded in taking over China. They felt he would have faded into obscurity if Mao hadn't used Norman as a political tool to urge the people on to greater selflessness.

Supporters argued that Norman couldn't possibly have seen into the future or known about the starvation. They pointed out that he helped people and saved lives; regardless of his political opinion, he was a humanitarian.

If Norman had been around to defend himself, he would have leaped into the debate and argued passionately. He would also have been pleased to see that his countrymen could be stirred out of complacency after all.

Whatever people think about Dr. Norman Bethune's ideology and motives, he was an ingenious and dedicated doctor. He treated all lives equally and fought to bring the same level of medical care to all Canadians — something we are still struggling with today.

Bibliography

Allan, Tony. *The Long March: The Making of Communist China.* Heinemann Library, 2001.

Broadfoot, Barry. *Ten Lost Years: Memories of Canadians Who Survived the Depression.* McClelland & Stewart Inc., 1997.

DuVernet, Sylvia. *The Muskoka Tree: poems of pride for Norman Bethune.* Bracebridge, Herald Gazette Press, 1976.

Gordon, Sydney & Allan, Ted. *The Scalpel, the Sword: The Story of Doctor Norman Bethune.* Monthly Review Press, 1973.

Hannant, Larry. *The Politics of Passion: Norman Bethune's Writing and Art.* University of Toronto Press, 1998.

Howard, Victor and Reynolds, Mac. *The Mackenzie-Papineau Battalion: The Canadian Contingent in the Spanish Civil War.* Carleton University Press Inc., 1986.

Hyde, Margaret O. *Know About Tuberculosis.* Walker and Company, 1994.

Bibliography

Jack, Donald. *Rogues, Rebels and Geniuses: The Story of Canadian Medicine*. Doubleday Canada Limited, 1981.

Landau, Elaine. *Tuberculosis*. Franklin Watts, 1995.

MacLeod, Wendell; Park, Libbie & Ryerson, Stanley. *Bethune: The Montreal Years*. James Lorimer, 1978.

Shephard, David A.E. & Levesque, Andrée. *Norman Bethune: His Times and His Legacy*. Ottawa: Canadian Public Health Association, 1982.

Smith, Mary Larratt. *Prologue to Norman: The Canadian Bethunes*. Mosaic Press/Valley Editions, 1976.

Stewart, Roderick. *The Mind of Norman Bethune*. Fitzhenry & Whiteside, 2002.

Stewart, Roderick. *The Canadians: Norman Bethune*. Fitzhenry & Whiteside Limited, 1974.

Stewart, Roderick. *Bethune*. New Press, 1973.

Webb, Michael. *Norman Bethune: Doctor Under Fire*. Copp Clark Pitman, 1993.

Wilson, John. *Righting Wrongs: The Story of Norman Bethune*.

Napoleon Publishing, 2001.

Wilson, John. *Norman Bethune: A Life of Passionate Conviction.* XYZ Publishing, 1999.

Zuehlke, Mark. *The Gallant Cause: Canadians in the Spanish Civil War.* Whitecap Books, 1996.

Appendix A
Bethune Ancestry

Norman Bethune was proud of his ancestry. He could trace it back to 16th century France when a family of Huguenots moved across the English Channel to settle in Scotland, where they could practise their Protestant religion without persecution. They were nonconformists, even then. They settled on the Isle of Skye, off the west coast of Scotland, and produced a line of feisty adventurers.

Angus Bethune: 1724–?
Norman's great, great, great grandfather fought in the famous Jacobite rebellion – at The Battle of Culloden – in an attempt to bring the Catholic Bonnie Prince Charlie to the English throne. The Jacobites were defeated and Angus was left for dead on the battlefield. When the English soldiers had left the bloodied field, Angus managed to crawl away. He made his way back to Skye, where he married Christina Campbell. Their son was John Bethune.

The Reverend John Bethune: 1750–1815
Reverend John and his relatives were forced out of Scotland by the English during a political manoeuvre known as the Highland Clearances. They immigrated to North Carolina, America, where they promptly raised a regiment called the Royal Highland Immigrants. They joined forces with other

royalists and fought for the Crown in the Revolutionary War. John, chaplain of the regiment, was captured. His plantation was confiscated and he was thrown into prison. Upon release, he rejoined his regiment and moved to Lower Canada (present-day Quebec). Here, the regiment helped General Montgomery defend the citadel against the Americans in 1775-76.

John went on to found the first Church of Scotland in Lower Canada and, later, the first Presbyterian church in Upper Canada (present-day Ontario). He had a reputation as a devoted man who cared deeply for his parishioners. He married Veronique Waddin; their first son was Angus Bethune.

Angus Bethune: 1783–1858

The oldest of nine children, Angus grew up in Montreal and then Charlottenburg, Glengarry County. His father was a good friend of the well-known explorer Alexander Mackenzie and the fur trader Alexander Henry. Inspired by these men, young Angus became a fur trader. He was barely 30 when he was made a partner in the North West Company. He travelled to China twice for the company, attempting to establish a market for furs.

These voyages must have been perilous, but perhaps not as dangerous as travelling in Canada in those days. During his constant travels, he stopped at the prairie settlement of Fort Vermilion. While he was in the fort, it was surrounded by warring Piegans and Assiniboines. He managed to escape to tell the tale.

He and his companions made many dangerous canoe voyages transporting furs. They left from Fort George, on the

Columbia River, and travelled through the Rocky Mountains to Fort William on Lake Superior (in present-day Ontario).

He later took charge of the new Hudson's Bay trading post at Sault Ste. Marie. He married a woman of Native ancestry; their second son was Norman Bethune.

Norman Bethune: 1822–1892

The first Dr. Norman Bethune attended King's College in Toronto, then studied medicine in London and Edinburgh. He married a young Scottish woman, Janet Nicholson, and returned to Toronto to set up a medical faculty in Trinity College. He resigned when non-Anglicans were barred from the college, and later founded Trinity College Medical School. This institute of learning admitted students without regard for their religious backgrounds.

He had a distinguished medical career teaching and practising medicine in Toronto. His wife died while their four children were still young, so he took them to Scotland to be brought up by Scottish relatives. During subsequent travels in Italy, he came upon the aftermath of the Battle of Solferino. Here he helped a well-known doctor, Henry Dunant, operate on injured soldiers. This experience spurred Dunant to found the Red Cross Society, earning him the first Nobel Peace Prize.

Norman eventually brought his two sons back to Canada. His younger son was Malcolm Bethune.

Malcolm Nicholson Bethune: 1857–1932

Malcolm, like his forbears, had wanderlust. He spent several years in Australia but couldn't find work. He went on to Hawaii, where he intended to grow oranges commercially.

However, he met Elizabeth Ann Goodwin. She persuaded him to return to Canada and go into the ministry of the Presbyterian Church. He followed her advice, attending Knox College. Malcolm and Elizabeth married in Toronto and had three children. Their older son was Henry Norman Bethune, otherwise known as Dr. Norman Bethune — Canada's rebel doctor.

Appendix B
Chronology of the Spanish Civil War

1919 Benito Mussolini founds the Fascist Party in Italy

1922 After using force and intimidation against opponents, Mussolini takes power, dissolves parliament, and forms a dictatorship.

1931 Spain is a monarchy. Landowners, the military, and the Catholic Church have great power. The working class agitates for self-government. A Republican government is elected in April and King Alphonse XIII of Spain chooses to go into exile. The government's reforms are too radical for the right wing, but not radical enough for some left wing groups.

1933 A centre-right wing government is elected. In protest, left wing partisans organize strikes. The army, led by General Francisco Franco, is called in to quell the strikes and riots. Franco's tactics are so brutal that public opinion swings back to the left.

In Germany, Adolf Hiltler becomes Chancellor. He suppresses opposition and brings the Nazis to power.

1936 In July, the military rises against the democratically elected government. Franco seizes power and civil war ensues. Franco asks Hitler and Mussolini for aid. Seeing him as a fellow Fascist, they agree. Approximately two-thirds of the Spanish population supports the Republicans; they flee to Republican-held areas. The rest of the world watches this first major military confrontation between left wing forces and Fascists with apprehension.

Canada passes The Foreign Enlistment Act making it illegal for volunteers to fight in the Spanish Civil War. (Canadian veterans of the International Brigades in Spain are later denied veteran status and are not allowed to serve in Canada's armed forces during WWII.)

August: Bombing of Madrid begins. Canadian Mac-Pap battalion is formed.

October: Russia sends aid to the Republicans. German and Italian bombers begin nightly raids on Madrid to destroy civilian resistance.

November: Expecting Madrid to fall, the Republican government moves to Valencia. Dr. Bethune arrives in Spain and establishes the Canadian Blood Transfusion Service.

1937 Malaga falls to the Nationalists in February and Almeria is bombed.

May: Dr. Bethune returns to Canada. He tours Canada and the U.S. on a speaking tour to raise funds for the Republican cause.

November: Republican government moves from Valencia to Barcelona.

1938 The International Brigades are disbanded in November.

1939 Republican Barcelona surrenders in January
February: Republican Catalonia surrenders
March: Republican Madrid surrenders and Valencia falls. 100,000 refugees flee the country.
April: General Franco declares the war is over. Republicans are jailed. His Fascist party remains in power until his death in 1975.
September: Having formed an alliance with Mussolini, Hitler invades Poland. Britain and France declare war on Germany; World War II begins.

1975 In Spain, Juan Carlos I becomes king and establishes a constitutional monarchy.

Author Note:
Norman Bethune and other active anti-Fascists repeatedly warned that unchecked Fascism would soon run rampant. When World War II broke out, history proved them correct.

Appendix C
Chronology of the Sino-Japanese War

1893 Mao Zedong is born to a well-to-do peasant family in Hunan Province.

1911 The republican forces of Sun Yat-sen launch the overthrow of the Manchu dynasty. Mao Zedong, now a student, becomes a radical political activist.

1912 The Last Emperor, Pu Yi, abdicates. This ends imperial rule in China.

1916 The warlord era begins.

1921 The Chinese Communist Party (CCP) is organized in Shanghai. Mao is a founding member and leader of the Hunan branch. The CCP forms a united front with Sun Yat-sen's republican followers, the Guomindang (Nationalists).

1925 The "Father of the Chinese Revolution," Sun Yat-sen, dies.

1926 Chiang Kai-shek, now in control of the Guomindang,

launches his "Northern Expedition" to raise support for the Nationalists.

1927 Chiang purges all Communists from the Nationalist movement. This period becomes known as the "White Terror." Mao flees to the countryside and, with Chu Teh, defends his rural base with a guerrilla army.

1931 Chiang launches the first Annihilation Campaign against the Communists.

Japanese forces occupy Manchuria.

1933 Chiang launches his fifth Annihilation Campaign against the Communists.

1934 Mao, now chairman of a soviet (a base area), leads his soldiers on The Long March to escape Chiang's soldiers.

1935 During the march, Mao is elected Communist Party Chairman. The Long March ends in Shaanxi province.

1936 Communists set up headquarters in Yan'an.

1937 Japanese invade southern China: The Sino-Japanese War begins.

1938 Chiang retreats from the Japanese, westwards to Sichuan.

February: Dr. Bethune and Jean Ewan leave Hankou for Yan'an.

March: Dr. Bethune meets Mao in Yan'an.

September: Dr. Bethune opens a model hospital in Songyankou.

October: Dr. Bethune begins training mobile medical units.

He is now medical advisor to the Jin-Cha-Ji Border Region.

1939 Britain and France declare war on Germany on September 3.

Canada declares war six days later.

Dr. Bethune's second model hospital is completed in Niuyankou.

November: Dr. Bethune dies of septicemia. His body is later moved to lie in state at Zhucheng.

1941 Nationalists and Communists break their truce in January.

December: Japanese attack Pearl Harbor.

The United States declares war on Japan.

1945 World War II ends. Japan is defeated and withdraws from China.

1946 Full-scale civil war resumes between Nationalists and Communists. Nationalists capture Communist capital of Yan'an. Nationalists are defeated in Manchuria.

1949 Beijing falls to the Communists. Mao proclaims the People's Republic of China. Chiang Kai-Shek resigns. He and the Nationalists agree to leave China. They go to Formosa

(Taiwan) where they set up their exiled government. Chiang rules this government in exile, waiting for a chance to control the mainland. His successors remain in control of Taiwan.

1952 Dr. Bethune's body is moved to a memorial park in Shijiazhuang.

His model hospital, now the Norman Bethune International Peace Hospital, is rebuilt in Shijiazhuang.

1966 Mao begins the Cultural Revolution.

1976 Chairman Mao Zedong dies. He is succeeded by Deng Xiaoping.

Acknowledgments

I would like to thank Norman Bethune's biographers for sparking my interest in the doctor and helping me to understand the kind of person he was. They are listed in the bibliography.

The poem "Red Moon," written by Dr. Bethune, was first published in *The Canadian Forum* in 1937. Dr. Bethune's essay "Wounds" was published in left-wing publications in 1939. Dr. Bethune's report about the bombing of refugees in Almeria was first published by Publicaciones Iberia in 1937. His description of Yan'an appeared in the *Daily Clarion* in 1938. I am also grateful for the services provided by our National Archives and the Calgary Public and University Libraries.

Thanks must also go to Altitude Publishing for giving me the opportunity to write this book, and editor Pat Kozak, who made me work hard when I thought the hard part was over — to the benefit of the finished book.

Writer friends Joan Dixon, Lisa Murphy-Lamb, Cathy Beveridge, and Sherile Reilly provided some much appreciated support, as did my immediate family: Keith, Claire, Adrienne, and Ian.

About the Author

Frances Hern grew up in Birmingham, England, and moved to Calgary, Alberta, with her husband in 1973. She has lived in Calgary ever since. As a child, Frances loved Saturday visits to the local library with her parents, and wrote poems and verses for homemade greeting cards. It wasn't until she had three children to share her favourite books with that she realized she wanted to write books as well as read them.

Frances has had numerous articles published, and a short story and poem will be published by Scholastic Canada in the spring of 2005. *Norman Bethune* is her first book.

Photo Credits

KLONDIKE JOE BOYLE
The Globetrotting Adventures of a Fearless Canadian Spy

*"...man with the heart of a Viking
and the simple faith of a child."*
Joe Boyle epitaph

An adventurer and a natural leader, Joe Whiteside Boyle blazed the White Pass to the Yukon and was among the few who scratched a fortune from the Klondike. During World War I, he was a spymaster working behind Russian lines. He cheated death many times to become the "Saviour of Rumania," and in the process fell in love with a queen.

 True stories. Truly Canadian.

ISBN 1-55153-969-1

PIERRE ELLIOTT TRUDEAU
The Fascinating Life of Canada's Most Flamboyant Prime Minister

"To a rapt national television audience, the soft-spoken minister with the Caesar-style haircut calmly justified his bill, saying, 'the State has no place in the bedrooms of the nation.'"

Pierre Trudeau was unlike any prime minister Canada had ever known or will ever see again. His unique style, charisma, bravado, and sharp wit galvanized a nation, creating the "Trudeaumania" that swept him into office. He was a man that Canadian's either loved or hated.

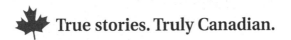 True stories. Truly Canadian.

ISBN 1-55153-945-4

AMAZING STORIES™

UNSUNG HEROES OF THE ROYAL CANADIAN AIR FORCE

Incredible Tales of Courage and
Daring During World War II

HISTORY

by Cynthia J. Faryon

UNSUNG HEROES OF THE ROYAL CANADIAN AIR FORCE
Incredible Tales of Courage and Daring During World War II

"That he was a hero is merely incidental to the fact that he died in pain — that he was robbed of life — and that he is lost to his generation. There is glory in living for an ideal as well as in dying for it."
Hector Bolitho, 1946

More than 250,000 courageous men and women were enlisted in the Royal Canadian Air Force during World War II. These Canadians fought valiantly in every major air operation from the Battle of Britain to the bombing of Germany. Thousands lost their lives. Those who survived to tell their stories were forever changed. Here are some of their incredible stories.

 True stories. Truly Canadian.

ISBN 1-55153-977-2

OTHER AMAZING STORIES

These titles are available wherever you buy books. If you have trouble finding the book you want, call the Altitude order desk at 1-800-957-6888, e-mail your request to: orderdesk@altitudepublishing.com or visit our Web site at www.amazingstories.ca

New AMAZING STORIES titles are published every month. If you would like more information, e-mail your name and mailing address to: amazingstories@altitudepublishing.com.